V-A-C-A-T-I-O-N

Cautionary Tales of Travelling Without Style

by

Oliver Gray

Sarsen Press

Winchester, UK

Following the international success of his first memoir, *VOLUME - A Cautionary Tale of Rock and Roll Obsession,* Oliver Gray now presents his gruesome reminiscences of a lifetime spent in the fruitless search for a successful holiday.

This book will appeal to anyone who has ever travelled anywhere. So that's you, then.

Oliver Gray's travel writings have appeared in many publications, including the *Independent on Sunday,* the *Times Educational Supplement,* the *Western Daily Press* and the *Hampshire Chronicle.*

Design: David Eno and Judith Blake
Cover photo: Sharon Armstrong-Williams
Cover design: Richard Williams for Pacific Hill
Printed by: Sarsen Press, 22, Hyde Street, Winchester, SO23 7DR, UK
Published by Sarsen Press
Copyright: Oliver Gray, 2001

Contact Oliver Gray at **P.O. Box 71, Winchester SO21 1ZE, UK**
Email: oliver@revilolang.demon.co.uk
www.olivergray.com

ISBN: 1-897609-37-X

CONTENTS

Cautionary Note
This book does not necessarily behave in a chronological manner. Bits just sort of merge into each other. You'll get used to it.
Dedication
To the women in my life, again: Birgit, Annabel, Lucy, Marble, Toffee, Smartie, Wotsit, Twiglet and Sugar. Next time, it WILL be a novel.
Thanks to:
Judith Blake, Paul Dominy, David Eno, Tony Hill, Richard Williams and loads of other people.
Special thanks to the **Rough Guides** and **Roger Walker Travel.**

Chapter 1.

V - A - C - A - T - I - O - N

"V - A - C - A - T - I - O - N". It's the title of quite a jolly song by Connie Francis. You sing the letters individually in the chorus.

The nearest English equivalent would be Cliff Richard's "Summer Holiday", but if you converse with Americans on such matters, you must remember to say "vacation" and not "holiday", otherwise they won't understand you.

Vacations, schmacations. Holidays, schmolidays. Just what are they?

If you like sitting on beaches doing sod all, stop reading here. No, hang on, don't stop just yet. Instead, buy the book and read it on the beach, congratulating yourself that you haven't had to experience all the horrors which the book contains. And I'll reciprocate by congratulating myself on not having to sit on the beach with you. I'd hate to do that. Nothing personal, it's just that I hate sitting on beaches.

It may therefore seem paradoxical that I recently planned the "Holiday of a Lifetime", namely a (very) belated honeymoon on a Caribbean island. But I was only prepared to do that because it appeared to be a practically uninhabited Caribbean island with no chance of any tourists. Whatsoever. I hate tourists. Even when I'm being one, I look down on them and would never consider myself to be one of them. Or, if I suspect I may actually be one, I look down on myself.

We once went on a package holiday. It was the worst few days of my life. What had happened was that we had done without a summer holiday, on account of a slight case of pregnancy. But now the infant had arrived, and we felt that we deserved a treat.

Majorca is sunny and nice, even in the winter, we were assured. Bollocks. Majorca is disgusting at any time of the year. Every so often, people write articles about how lovely and unspoilt the "rest of" Majorca is. Oh yeah? Anywhere which can have such revolting bits can't possibly have enough in the way of redeeming features. True, it might similarly be argued that no parts of Scotland can be beautiful in view of the existence of East Kilbride, but the comparison is not apt. Why? Because I'm not prejudiced against Scotland.

The hotel was in Santa Ponsa. This sounded good, like some kind of outlaw character from the Magnificent Seven. At the airport, however, we had to get on a coach full of Midlands pensioners and the alarm bells should have rung then. But I was too busy being appalled by the view from the windows. The view was of mid-winter Magaluf.

You hear about Magaluf occasionally on the news, normally because some UK tourist has been murdered there in a brawl. Yep, that makes sense. It is easy to comprehend anyone being driven to murder in such a vile place. Only one thing could be uglier than the closed-down concrete discos, bars and chip shops I saw through the glass: the same scene populated by Bermuda-shorted, pissed up, aggressive drunks. That's what it's like in the summer, I'm reliably assured. I don't wish to know.

Off-season Bognor or Clacton would be preferable to the not-Mexican-bandit-like-at-all metropolis of Santa Ponsa. The hotel had all the character of a Basingstoke tower block and, yes, we had to share a table with two pensioner couples from Solihull. They tried to make conversation, but it was impossible, mainly because I immediately switched into "I refuse to attempt to make conversation with pensioners from Solihull" mode. Plus, they pretended to love our baby but looked disapproving the moment she did anything baby-like, such as crying, dribbling or puking.

We'd opted for full board, which in one way was lucky, because all Santa Ponsa's restaurants were closed for the winter. In another way, it was unlucky, because it was a help-yourself buffet which didn't seem to adjust itself to any particular mealtime. Everything tasted of some kind of preservative and the entire canteen-like room had that McDonalds type of sick-making aroma caused by people squirting mildly scented disinfectant all over every surface. I surmised that they must have vats of the various dishes out the back and merely replenish the buffet occasionally. Surely this was a recipe for food poisoning?

It was. Agonising, sweat-pouring, "I'll teach you to tempt me" style food poisoning. You want details? Tough. I can't even spell diarroeah, far less describe it.

We'd booked and paid for a hire car, but it simply didn't appear. No amount of pidgin phone calls could make it materialise, so we spent a lot of time on manically-driven buses careering along unmade-up roads between the uncompleted tower blocks. Some of the potholes were so huge that the infant Annabel was nearly hurled out of the pouch in which I held her; I had to rest my chin on her head to prevent her from being ejected like a stricken fighter pilot.

We did exciting things like breast-feeding Annabel in a corner of a department store (well, I didn't do it personally, but I stood around interestedly). Unlike the English, who would either have averted their eyes or tut-tutted, the Majorcans, attracted by her - to them - unusual blonde hair, lined up to watch the operation.

On the evening of January 6th, it being the Festival of Kings, there was to be a carnival procession. It was a bit of a damp squib, unlike the activities of the local rocket-launcher squad.

How would you launch a rocket? Presumably, like me, you'd place it carefully in a bottle, light the blue touch paper, withdraw rapidly and get ready to say "Whooo!"

The inebriated young men of Santa Ponsa had other ideas. Their launching method was to insert the rockets under their armpits, light them and propel them horizontally into the crowd. We had Annabel in a buggy and I literally enveloped the entire vehicle in my body. You can blast my eyes out, mateys, but you don't hurt my baby. That's the nearest I get to being macho.

So that did it for me and package tours. The very thought of them makes my flesh creep. I'm not even tempted by things like Center Parcs, because they are designed with no intention other than to take my money. I love holidays doing and experiencing things that originally had some other purpose, but a place which serves no other function apart from giving you a holiday ... no, sorry.

I suppose things might be different if I'd been brought up on "proper" holidays, but I wasn't. We didn't really have holidays at all. I have a vague memory of my mother taking me, as an infant, to stay with some relations at Saunton Sands in Devon. The man was a fat, red-faced vicar who flew into rages for no particular reason. I don't think he liked children, because I still retain a picture of a florid, spittle-adorned visage screaming into my face from a distance of about two inches. There were tufts of grey, bristly hair on his cheeks where he hadn't shaved properly, and little red veins on his nose. I remember that, but of Saunton Sands I have no memory at all.

The reason we didn't have holidays was that my father was an amateur archaeologist. This meant that every summer was spent hunched down holes in the middle of a field near Frocester in Gloucestershire, excavating a Roman villa. I was supposed to be interested in this, but I wasn't. There were no girls and very little excitement, unless excavating Roman villas excites you. To be fair, plenty of the people who worked there found it tremendously exciting, but to a teenager who had no interest in history, it wasn't the most thrilling way to spend the summer.

One thing which seemed extraordinary was how very careless the Romans appeared to have been with their money. Every couple of hours, someone would find a coin. Everyone would gather round and examine it, before the retired naval captain who ran the operation would march over, confiscate the coin and take it back to his shed for analysis. No one else was ever allowed into the shed and the coins never reappeared.

The first time I found a coin, I remember being delirious with excitement. Well, come on, it feels good even when you find a penny on the floor of the pub, doesn't it? The other excavators gathered round admiringly and the good captain appeared within moments, snatching my coin and shouting at me in an uncontrolled way because I had scratched it with my trowel. Oddly enough, he, too, had sticking-out red veins, grey bristles and wayward spittle.

For good measure, he emerged from his shed a short time later to announce that in any case, it had been a coin of negligible significance, scratched or un-scratched. None of the coins seemed

8

to be at all important, and it appeared that the careless Romans had carried purses consisting entirely of holes.

The other thing that we found all the time were little blocks of stone called Tesserae. The Romans had made their floors out of thousands of these miniature tiles, so finding the occasional one wasn't that much of a big deal. But for the good captain, they were enough to send him into paroxysms of joy. He also got excited by tiny bits of broken pot, on the basis of which he would draw pictures of what he thought the pot must originally have looked like. After a while I decided he was mad, and that he was also purposely planting the coins, rather like you do with a Christmas pudding. Probably there was only one, which was permanently recycled. If all the coins we found had been kept, the captain would surely have been a millionaire, even if each one had only been worth a penny.

One day, my father announced that he was going to take me on a walking tour in Wales. I think he felt that this would be a bonding experience, but it didn't particularly turn out to be so. The plan was to walk along Offa's Dyke, which sounded spectacular in theory, but in practice wasn't a lot more than a slightly elevated footpath. Every now and then, we would do detours to places with rather sweet little castles on mounds. One of these was called Clun, which even then struck me as sounding like some obscure female body part, as in, "Cor, look at the cluns on that!"

All went reasonably well until we reached a place called Newtown (of which there must be hundreds, but this particular one was somewhere in the Welsh Borders). There, I contracted something which will become a bit of a *leit-motif* of this book, namely an upset stomach. Other people go to India to get food poisoning, I made it as far as Montgomeryshire. As a result, my abiding memory of this particular jaunt is of lying for two days in a darkened room in a B & B in Newtown. The reason for remembering it so clearly is the taste it brings to my mouth of Milk of Magnesia, the medicine my father chose with which to attack the problem.

To make Milk of Magnesia, you steal some white chalk from your local school, crush it to powder with a pestle and mortar and stuff it up your nose, no, sorry, you mix it with water and drink it by the tablespoonful. This recipe may in fact be flawed, but you would achieve the identical taste. It did, to be fair, work quite effectively and before long I had recovered. But by then it was time to go home.

The following year, flushed with the relative success of the Welsh operation, Father decided he was going to take me to France. For unknown reasons, he booked us for a week into a guest house called "Les Glycines" in a town near Paris called Mantes-La-Jolie. Considering that *jolie* means *pretty*, this is a misnomer, since it is now one of the notorious *banlieus* of Paris, consisting of vast concrete estates which are hotbeds of social unrest. But back then, it was just a boring little town.

Father was delighted when it turned out that the owner had a young son of about my age. Unfortunately, we both took an instant dislike to one another and the poor lad was resentfully dragged round a selection of *châteaux* with us, because his parents also had the well-meaning notion that we might become friends and that he might be invited back to England. No chance. He dribbled. Well, I know that doesn't sound very pleasant, but the truth often isn't very pleasant.

The following summer, I was fifteen and deemed old enough to be sent, alone, on a French language course in Tours. This was much more appealing, because this university town had plenty of discos and cafés and I soon got used to drinking beer and smoking those revolting Gitanes which are wrapped in yellow bog paper. The teacher, a large, virtually senile old man, stood in front of the class and delivered lectures about French grammar of which we understood not a word. He, too, smoked the bog paper Gitanes all through the lessons, the browned stub permanently attached to his lower lip and the ash forming a light dusting on his enormous stomach. One can't begin to imagine what his lungs must have looked like.

I stayed as a lodger with a nice couple who had a smelly baby and lived in what I now realise was a slum, but at the time seemed quite romantic. It was an extremely old, half-timbered little house in a back street, smelling of drains, stale cooking and nappies, but when I threw open the shutters and looked down from my garret onto the street below, I felt quite important as I waved to the passers-by. It was the first time in my life that I had my "own" room.

Many years later, I set out on a mission to find that little house and see what had become of the family. I walked the back streets of Tours for hours before reluctantly admitting what I didn't want to admit: that the entire area had been bulldozed and replaced by deadly Mantes-La-Jolie style tower blocks.

The only family holiday we we ever had was an unusual and excellent one. Nostalgic for the wartime days they had spent there (my father having been stationed in Lerwick as an Intelligence Officer), my parents took me and my two sisters on a cruising tour of the Orkneys and Shetlands.

If the term "cruise" conjures up the idea of sharing the captain's table for dinner on a luxury liner, leaning romantically on the railing as the sun sets over a crystal blue sea, then this was no cruise. Instead, we joined a small, frighteningly unstable tramp steamer which delivered post, provisions and even livestock round the various islands. But first, it had to get us from Aberdeen to Kirkwall in Orkney, which entailed crossing the notorious Pentland Firth in a force nine gale. As each gigantic wave approached, the boat would rear up over the top of it before plunging vertically down the other side, just in time for the bows to be almost completely submerged under the next approaching wave.

I stood behind some glass windows towards the front of the boat, transfixed by its ability not to sink. I was, however, convinced that it eventually would, so drifted into that oddly resigned state of mind which says, okay, I'm going to die shortly, there's nothing I can do about it, so I might as well just appreciate what little time I have left. Throughout all this, neither I, my parents or my sisters felt even the tiniest bit seasick. In fact, to this day, I have never been seasick. Okay, it's not much of a talent to boast about, but it's a gift that not everyone has.

I think the "cruise" lasted a couple of weeks, visiting the islands one by one, but mostly not getting off because the ship couldn't dock. We did get to talk to one lady on one of the remoter islands and my father politely asked her how often she went to Lerwick, the small town which is the capital of the Shetlands. "Not very often," she replied. "I don't like the Big City".

I made friends with the son of the ship's engineer and spent quite a lot of time in the engine room, watching his father shovelling coal into the furnace in the sweltering heat. This was not a job I aspired to, although I'd have loved to have had a go at operating the boom crane which winched cows, legs dangling and heads lolling gormlessly, from the ship, over the water and onto the wooden landing stages.

So that was it. No real holidays at all, at least none in the form in which they appear in travel brochures. But when I was sixteen, my friends and I had our first parent-less adventure. It didn't last long, but it was fun - sort of - while it lasted. Someone dreamed up the idea of going camping in Porthcawl. Wales again. I've no idea why, it just happened. At the time, I had an exchange "partner" over from Germany. Called Johann, he was a year older than me and was already into things such as music, girls and pubs which were strictly off the menu in the unexciting little village where I lived. He was bored rigid, something which became more than obvious when I returned and spent time with him and his family in Germany.

"How was it in England?" his friends would ask, mildly jealous of the fact that Johann had visited the land of mini-skirts, the Beatles and Swinging London, all of them sadly absent from the range of experience we offered him. Of course, I secretly hoped that he would say *"toll"* or *"dufte"* or some other German word which I would recognise as meaning "great". But he always replied, *"Es war okay."*

"But what about the time when we went off to Wales without my parents?" I would ask. "That was '*toll*', wasn't it?"

"Hmmm ... Es war okay."

Admittedly, the few days of wild freedom hadn't worked out precisely as planned. For a start, despite the fact that it was July, it pissed with rain the entire time. My friend Roger's father dropped us four lads off at the campsite and we erected our tents, two of us in each, plus a "provisions" tent. We had a Primus stove, one of those infuriating devices which you had to pump for hours and with extreme difficulty before anything resembling a flame would emerge. It could take an entire morning to make a cup of tea.

As we pumped the Primus in the tent on the first evening, some methylated spirit landed on my shoe and caught fire. Like something from the Towering Inferno, I hopped around with the flames emitting from my feet, screaming in terror, until I discovered that it didn't do any damage at all. All that happened was that the spirit burned but the shoe remained intact. This was such a novelty that we all took it in turns to pour methylated spirit over various parts of our bodies and charge around making the other astonished campers think we were suffering from third degree burns. Well, you had to be there.

In the morning, we woke to discover that the provisions tent had blown away. There was no sign of it at all. The provisions were still in situ, neatly piled up but unfortunately suffering somewhat from the torrential storm which had occurred during the night. There's actually something rather sensual about picking up a waterlogged toilet roll and squeezing it until the juice runs down your ... oh, you get the Led Zeppelinesque picture. Luckily, the baked beans were unaffected, so we weren't going to starve, even though we had to wipe our bottoms on rather scratchy reeds which we harvested from the dunes.

So we set off to explore. To get to the beach, we inconveniently had to walk right through the middle of a golf course, actually, I think, the Royal Porthcawl, which you occasionally hear mentioned in sports bulletins. It was a dangerous business, not only on account of the high-velocity projectiles whistling past our heads, but also because of the furious tempers of the posh but intolerant golfers, who would wave their clubs at us and shout things like "Fore!" and "You're trespassing!". In fact, we were merely following one of those wooden signs saying "Footpath", but they didn't think we should. Being youngsters, we didn't actually qualify, to golfers, as members of the human race.

When we finally stumbled through the dunes onto the beach, we realised that there wasn't really much to do there, so repaired to the town, where we found quite a lively fairground, as well as a café which I swear had an early prototype of the concept of a video juke box. It played 45 rpm singles along with a flickering, out of synch reel of Super Eight film. I know for a fact that I saw The Hollies playing "(Ain't That) Just Like Me" on that machine.

As dusk approached, we walked round and round the fairground, too poor to actually go on any rides (which would have made us ill anyway) and trying with minimal success to look "hard". This attracted the attention of a small gaggle of girls, who started to follow us around, giggling and winking. Unfortunately, we also attracted the attention of a gang of local bequiffed teddy boys who, displeased that the girls were displaying interest in us rather than in them, chased us off the fairground and along the beach, brandishing bicycle chains and flick knives. Well, I don't think they had either, actually, but these essential items belonged to the image of teddy boys, so that's what we told our friends afterwards.

I may sound blasé about this now, but at the time I was genuinely in fear of my life. I crouched, shivering, in the lee of a sand dune in the dark until I was quite sure that the search had been given up. And then I waited a bit longer, in the unlikely fear that they were intelligent enough to remain quiet in order to flush us out.

During the night, both our other tents blew away. We woke to find we were as exposed and sodden as our pathetic-looking provisions. Considering that it would be a matter of extreme physical danger to remain anywhere near Porthcawl, we phoned Roger's dad and he came and picked us up again.

Now I think of it, it's little wonder that Johann refused to concede that it had been anything more than "okay".

Chapter 2

Nothing Like a Fahrt

Like "*Auspuff*", the German word "*Fahrt*" causes intense amusement to English people. So let's get it straight. It means "journey". And nothing else.

I hadn't been expecting to embark on any "*Fahrts*" when I arrived in Germany with Johann. The idea was for me to improve my German, and I was immediately introduced into life at the Gymnasium Anna Sophianium, the local grammar school in the small town of Schöningen, just by the border with East Germany. It was a sweltering summer and the only thing I remember about Johann's father, the local bank manager, was that he poured with sweat the whole time. It literally tumbled off his face like a waterfall. One wipe was sufficient to completely saturate a whole hanky. He carried a bag full of these around with him all the time, hanging them out to dry on the balcony.

Johann's mother, meanwhile, liked to tell me her troubles. Sometimes, Johann would have extra lessons in the afternoon and I would go home and sit on the balcony while his mother, in a starched white smock, would do the ironing, ply me with endless supplies of apple juice mixed with sparkling water (neither tasty nor refreshing) and ask my advice about everything. Considering that I only understood about twenty percent of what she said, this was challenging, but I tried. It was mainly about Johann. His school marks weren't very good and there was a chance that he might have to "*sitzenbleiben*" (meaning repeat a school year), which he had already done once, meaning that he was already a year older than everyone else in his class. But he spent the whole time playing his guitar and (this seemed to trouble her greatly) he had no girlfriend. What was my advice?

This was difficult. I could hardly tell her the truth, which was that he wasn't very bright. So I just reassured her that everything would turn out all right in the end.

The school was just magnificent. One of the great mysteries of European life is why it is that the German education system is so much more successful that everyone else's, in view of the fact that they do so little work. True, they start at a most disgraceful hour (normally 7.30 or 7.45), but by lunchtime, they've finished and gone home. They don't get much in the way of homework and there's little organised sport (hooray). But what they do have is extremely rigorous testing, and if you fail the tests, you've had it. You have to *"sitzenbleiben"*, and that carries with it such terror of humiliation that everyone works for the tests.

In the first week, I got invited into lots of English lessons, in order to to read aloud texts and be used as a pronunciation model. I was terribly popular, causing gales of uproarious laughter with my every ribald remark. Being tactless, immature and stupid, I kept putting my hand up and contradicting the teacher, correcting his grammar and pronunciation (for example, like most Germans, he said *"heppy"* instead of *"happy"* and *"cet"* instead of *"cat"*). Like a fool, I couldn't just leave him in peace, I had to try and get him to pronounce the words correctly, leaving him like a goldfish, unsuccessfully trying to get his mouth round a vowel sound he was never going to master. The pupils thought it was hysterical and, before the end of the first week, the inevitable happened: Johann's parents received a letter from the Headmaster, requesting that I should no longer attend school as I was having a disruptive influence on the children.

So instead, I took to spending the days just wandering round the town and through the fields that led towards the border with East Germany. There was such a peculiar atmosphere there. The only clue that anything was amiss was that you'd start noticing red and white signs which said *"Achtung: Zonengrenze"* and the more frightening *"Achtung: Minen"*. In this idyllic summer, you couldn't imagine the possibility of mines beneath the tall grass, but you could see the fences and the watchtowers in the distance. They were there to prevent people trying to escape to the West, but the guards nonetheless would observe me as I lay in the long grass, accompanied only by the sound of the crickets chirruping, and wondered what things were like beyond the mines and the impenetrable fence. I could tell the guards were watching me because the sunshine reflected off the lenses of their binoculars. In the knowledge that I was way beyond their jurisdiction, I would sit in the tall grass, being very brave as I flashed V-signs in their general direction. As this is not an internationally recognised mode of insult, it doubtless didn't make the guards tremble in their boots.

Some evenings, a gang of us teenagers would walk through the woods to the *Waldfrieden*, an isolated pub which manufactured its own cherry wine from fruit grown in its garden. This stuff was far too strong for an inexperienced young drinker like me, so the path back to Schöningen was liberally spattered with blood-red vomit in the style of Jackson Pollock. On one occasion, I fell so deeply asleep on a bench in the woods that Johann was incapable of waking me and simply left me there overnight. His parents seemed completely unfazed by this, let's face it, appalling behaviour.

So back to the *Fahrt*. This institution is one of the many wonderful things about German schools. Once a year, each class goes off somewhere for a week or ten days, in school time. This is supposed to be a bonding and educational experience, and it is, to the extent that doing bugger all with your mates for a week is bonding and educational. I'm all in favour.

Suddenly, it was announced that I had been invited to accompany the *"elfte Klasse"* on a *Fahrt*, to be precise, a *Frankenfahrt*. This didn't signify anything to me until I worked out that it meant we would be travelling on a coach round Franken, or Franconia, staying in Youth Hostels as we went. The *"elfte Klasse"* (eleventh class) was the next class up from Johann's, so I would be travelling with people a year older than me. And just like a week is a long time in politics, a year is a heck of a long time in your teens. What was more, the human Niagara which was Johann's father not only paid for the entire trip but also pressed a sodden fifty mark note into my hand as I departed. It might seem that they were trying to get rid of me but the fact was that they were just incredibly kind people.

The opportunity had cropped up more or less overnight, caused by someone falling ill, so I didn't really understand what was happening as we climbed on board a decrepit old bus and headed off towards who knew where? I should have felt intimidated by being with all these older people, but from the first moment, it was obvious that they were all extremely interested in me. Most Germans seemed to adore everything English, so a real live English boy was something to be fought over.

The first person to vie for my favours was a young man called Detlev. He was what my children would call a "boff", top of the class but also very funny. Although I didn't know it at the time, Detlev is the cliché German joke name for over-the-top camp men (rather like Julian and Sandy from "Round The Horne") and Detlev more than lived up to the stereotype. He had a lisp, a very high-pitched voice, an infectious giggle and a propensity to grab my arm enthusiastically at every opportunity. It never entered my head at the time, but he may well have had unformulated designs on me. As far as I was concerned, he was an extremely kind, friendly and, above all, hysterically funny person.

But somebody else wanted to be my friend. This was Knut, the opposite extreme to Detlev. Knut (pronounced Knoot) was muscle-bound, fashionably-dressed and keen to be associated with the token Englishman. The token Englishman didn't reciprocate, because Knut had a dramatic and pronounced personal hygiene problem. He stank of B.O., to the extent that the entire bus, despite all its windows being open, reeked exclusively of Knut's inimitably pungent sweat. Naturally, Knut wanted to sit next to me and it was difficult to find any way to decline his attention.

The *"elfte Klasse"* was overflowing with staggeringly beautiful girls. I wanted them to like me as well, but maybe they would think that the pong was emitting from me, rather than from Knut? But there was no need to worry, since they had known him and his affliction for years and liked to pinch their noses while pointing at him behind his back and giggling. Knut, naturally, remained blissfully unaware of this but couldn't understand why I took every opportunity to stand up and go to converse with people in other parts of the coach. It was unbearable. If you breathed through your nose, you got the full effect hitting you like an express train, but if you breathed through your mouth, you feared you might be damaging your health by inhaling the toxic emissions.

It's odd to think that the mere chance fact of being English could make you attractive, but that's invariably what happens when, as an English person, you visit Germany. This was my first experience of this pleasant phenomenon, and I soon learned to revel in it. The first girl who homed in on me was called Brigitte, and she didn't waste any time. We arrived at the first stop, an impossibly beautiful and unspoilt town called Coburg (actually, everywhere we went was impossibly beautiful and unspoilt) and checked into a youth hostel, which was actually a castle, rumoured to be haunted.

German youth hostels are largely kept going by the *Klassenfahrt* system, and at any given time are filled with groups of schoolchildren of various ages. The normal youth hostel rules apply in theory: You are supposed to wash up, have lights out at 10 pm and observe strict rules about segregation. In practice, most of these rules are ignored. In Coburg, the boys were allocated two dormitories full of bunks, but mysteriously, everyone from Knuts's room preferred to sleep on the floor of the other room rather than risk being asphyxiated in their sleep, and Knut slept in regal isolation.

The communal supper had been *Leberknödelsuppe*, which translates as Liver Dumpling Soup. I couldn't imagine what this might be, but youth hostels don't normally offer a choice of menu, so you were obliged to eat what you were given, or else starve. It turned out to be just what it said, a round thing made of liver and flour, nestling like an island in a bowl of clear chicken soup, adorned with parsley. It was lovely.

After supper, Brigitte took me by the hand and led me into the castle garden, a grassy ex-moat surrounded by high walls. In the moonlight, she looked up at me and instructed me to kiss her. But there was a problem. A stray piece of parsley had attached itself to Brigitte's lower lip and, glinting like a green jewel in the moonlight, was putting me off. I had little experience in these matters but was worried that the errant piece of herb might transfer itself to me. I wondered what to do and in the end, took the only possible course. I said:

"Brigitte, you have a piece of parsley attached to your lower lip. Please can I remove it before I kiss you?"

God knows what form of hesitant German words I must have used, but Brigitte seemed to think this was quite romantic.

"Of course you can," she said. "Go ahead."

So I raised my index finger to her mouth, detached the green blob, wiped it off on my trousers and kissed Brigitte as requested. But there wasn't much enthusiasm involved, because

(A) it was hardly what you would call spontaneous, and

(B) also on the *Fahrt* were Christa and Ute.

Christa and Ute were best friends and, in the time-honoured tradition of the Dirty Parrot Joke, one had beautiful long black hair and the other had beautiful long blonde hair. What? You don't know the Dirty Parrot Joke? Never mind, it isn't very funny anyway.

Both Christa and Ute had perfect complexions and big eyes which they used for flirting. They knew exactly how irresistible they were and how to reel in hopeless victims like me.

On the day after my moonlit vegetable manipulation with Brigitte, she was eager to demonstrate to her classmates that she had achieved the UK invasion which Hitler hadn't. She gripped my hand determinedly as we continued our guided tour of all things Coburgian, but as we re-mounted the coach, Christa applied the adhesive of her superglue eyes and patted the seat next to her. I was putty in her hands as I prised mine (my hand, I mean) from Brigitte's and placed myself next to Christa. This was one row from the back of the coach. Behind us sat Ute, resisting the attentions of Arno, an innocuous young man who was plainly in love with her.

Christa immediately placed her head on my shoulder and stared defiantly at Brigitte, who stood in the gangway of the coach, her face a mixture of fury, amazement and jealousy at the brazen behaviour of her old classmate and her new boyfriend. Me, I was powerless to do anything other than follow where I was led, which was into an all-day fumbling session with the glorious Christa. I just couldn't believe my luck.

As the week meandered on, we explored towns with names like Nürnberg, Würzburg, Fulda and Rothenburg ob der Tauber. The idyllic weather continued, and everywhere we went were romantic old castles, churches and museums, each complete with a guided tour featuring, in true German fashion, a never-ending listing of hundreds of statistics, dates and unwanted biographical details of the architects, the artists, the princes and the dukes. This just came as part of the deal, but we didn't have to make any notes or write any essays, so we merely stood and listened, letting all the information wash over us but not impinge on our general empty-headedness.

Of all the ridiculously beautiful places we visited, Rothenburg ob der Tauber was the most ridiculously beautiful, an ancient walled town whose defences were completely intact. We all walked all the way round the ramparts, taking about two hours. The walls were very narrow, with a little wooden roof, just like you imagine from stories by the Brothers Grimm. I suppose it was twee and escapist, but I thought I'd stumbled into fairyland and life seemed perfect.

As the coach pulled out of Rothenburg, I realised that the blonde vision of perfectitude which was Ute was applying her magnetic pupils and patting the seat next to her by the window in the back row. This seemed too good to be true, so I looked at Christa to see how she would react. She smiled at me, then at Ute, and nodded encouragingly. As I sat down next to Ute, not only Brigitte but also the hapless Arno looked daggers at me, but Christa didn't seem bothered at all, as if it was all part of some fairytale game plan. Arno sat by her and attempted to chat her up, but she merely looked out of the window and didn't respond.

Ute, meanwhile, put the head-on-shoulder manoeuvre into immediate operation and, because we were at the very back, and therefore unobserved, the journey to Fulda was uniquely educational.

*Rothenburg ob der Tauber, **aka** Fairyland*

Fulda was to be the last night of the *Fahrt*, so we had persuaded the teacher that we should have an end-of-journey party. Herr Müller, the remarkably long-suffering and tolerant Geography teacher who was in charge of us, and who had obviously spent untold hours preparing this wonderful trip for a largely disinterested and not particularly grateful clientèle, declared that we would all go out to a restaurant he knew in Fulda in order to sample the local *Frankenwein*.

But as we arrived at the Youth Hostel, yet another converted castle, this time a rather dingy-looking one in the middle of some dark woods, there was a nasty shock. We were awaited by the hostel warden, or *Herbergsvater*, enormously fat and very frightening, who pointed our way into a day room. Before we settled in, he said, he wished to say a few words.

Standards, he said, were known to be slipping in some of today's youth hostels. He wanted us to know that this was not the case here in Fulda. Rules were rules, and he wished to make it clear that he would not tolerate any transgressions. No alcohol of any kind was to be consumed, either on or off the premises. Any evidence of smoking would lead to exclusion. Regular patrols all night would ensure that under no circumstances would any boys enter the girls' dormitories or vice versa. And finally, there was a strict curfew of 10 pm, after which the hostel would be locked.

We listened, crestfallen and ashen-faced, realising that our plans to go out on a high were doomed.

In the evening, we walked quietly down the track through the woods and sat in the restaurant drinking Sinalco lemonade. The mood was sombre. Suddenly, Herr Müller had had enough. "You know what?" he said. "If he won't let us back in, we'll sleep in the coach. Why should he spoil our last evening?"

A huge cheer went up and several bottles of *Frankenwein* were immediately opened. By the time we left, well after midnight, Herr Müller and all the pupils, including me, of course, were blind drunk. But as we staggered back through the woods, reality began to impinge. What would await us back at the hostel?

As we rounded the last bend, the sinister silhouette of the hostel was illuminated only by the light emitting from the main door. Framed in the doorway was the huge figure of the *Herbergsvater*, obviously waiting for us. Suddenly feeling chilled and sober, we sheepishly shuffled towards the door, gradually becoming able to make out more details of the figure. It appeared ... could it be true ... that one hand held an enormous cigar, while the other clutched a three-quarters empty bottle of vodka. And he was smiling inanely as he swayed from side to side. We pinched ourselves.

"Welcome back!" he boomed. "Let's have a party!"

Bottles of *Frankenwein* appeared as if by magic, loud music was switched on, and a full-scale celebration ensured that our last night didn't finish until the early hours.

In the morning, I felt terrible, but the eternally reliable Christa and Ute were as calm and collected as ever, smiling sweetly as they installed themselves in the back seat and motioned to me to come and sit between them. Even the furious Brigitte and the multi-rejected Arno had found solace in each others' arms during the previous night.

There's nothing like a good *Fahrt*.

Chapter 3

Technical Hitch

Hitch-hiking. Even the term sounds a bit antiquated.

Somehow, the entire concept belonged to a more innocent era which is no longer with us. The vaguely hippyish notion of redistributing transport possibilities among the masses (well, okay, it wasn't that idealistic, but indulge me) couldn't possibly survive the "me" ideology which Margaret Thatcher introduced and now remains with us, seemingly for ever.

I used to hitch all the time. When still at school, I would hitch home and pocket the bus money. When at university, I know for a fact that the only time ever I didn't hitch from London to Norwich was the very first time, when a kind relative took me there with all my luggage. And I would undertake tortuous journeys to various obscure parts of the UK to visit friends. So it must have worked.

Always, when abandoned on some dusty Texas-style (in my imagination) highway, when a speck in the distance would turn into the imperious swishing-past of some expensive vehicle with only one person in it, as my head turned 180 degrees to follow it until it became a speck again, and as the unavoidable word "bastard" passed my lips, I swore to myself one thing, and I swore it with total belief and utter honesty: When I have enough money to buy a car, I will pick up hitch-hikers. Every time. Of that, there was no possible doubt.

Now, I don't pick up hitch-hikers. Ever. That's odd, isn't it? But even the Rough Guides' section on hitching is now reduced to a brief paragraph just saying "Don't".

When I was hitching, I expected to be picked up because I looked the part of the typical hitcher. I was scruffy and obviously not well-off, and thus had a good reason for hitching. Students hitch-hiked a lot, and that was an accepted fact. But if I had been short-haired and tidy, I'd have been an off-duty soldier on the way back to barracks, which wouldn't have posed any danger either.

And if I'd been middle-aged and carrying red number plates, I'd have been doing something to do with registering a car. All of us would have got a lift.

Actually, not too long ago, Birgit and I did pick up some hitchers. We were driving quite fast along the beautiful dual carriageway coast road between Dorchester and Bridport when we became aware that we had passed a forlorn-looking couple stranded in a spot where it was plain that no one would stop for them. Having passed them, we looked at each other. It was obvious that we would have to go back and get them.

What was it about them? It was a kind of bygone innocence. We applied the rules of stereotyping and concluded (correctly, there was no possibility of error) that they were Scandinavian. The boy was tall, bronzed, blonde, had blue eyes and steel-rimmed spectacles and looked completely innocent. The girl was tall, bronzed, blonde, had blue eyes and steel- rimmed spectacles and looked equally innocent. And they both wore baggy shorts and enormous rucksacks with cooking utensils dangling off them.

We had to drive quite a long way before it was possible to descend from the dual carriageway, re-mount the other side, return all the way back to the roundabout at Dorchester, turn round again and go back and pick them up. We knew for a fact that nobody would have given them a lift in the interim. I was convinced that they must have been having a shitty time trying to hitch round a suspicious and unwelcoming UK and I wanted them to tell their friends when they got home, "Well, at least there was this one really nice couple who picked us up in Dorset."

And so it was that, when they enquired whether we were going to a destination some ten miles beyond where we were actually headed, we both, without discussing it or even looking at each other, replied in the affirmative. We even drove off further down the same road after dropping them, to give them the impression that we hadn't gone out of our way, which might have embarrassed them. It was a wonderful, simultaneously uplifting and depressing Blast From The Past.

But now ... well, what is it exactly that has changed? Have we just become middle-aged and over-influenced by the media? Me, I fear the following things:

1. The scruffy, long-haired character hitching a ride may well be a peace-loving, impoverished student. But he might also be a junkie who plans to threaten me with a knife and steal my wallet in order to buy drugs.

2. The short-haired, well-dressed person might be an off-duty soldier, but he could also be a thuggish, racist skinhead who could well mug me.

3. The middle-aged man with the trade plates is most likely a paedophile on the run.

4. And, lest we forget the existence of female hitch-hikers, the attractive girl at the side of the road is probably going to falsely accuse me of rape and have me locked up.

So, if you want to hitch with success, what you must do is dress up as an innocent young Scandinavian. Except that you'll be such a sitting duck that the driver will probably abduct you and hold you to ransom.

The best advice I ever got about hitching was to try to appear honest. Apparently, the best way to appear honest is to look your potential lift-giver straight in the eye. It doesn't necessarily mean that you really are honest (many a fine performer who has convinced the punter in the front row that he or she is the performer's best friend will attest to that), but at least it makes you appear not to be shifty. It might even hold out to the driver the possibility of a pleasant and interesting conversation.

These were the rules I impressed upon my travelling companion Martin as we began to make our plans for a summer's hitch from Bremen, in North Germany, where we were working, to Southern Europe. It wasn't just that we couldn't afford to travel by some other method, more that we both felt in some idealistic way that the journey was more important than the destination. Maybe Spain, we thought. And, I blushingly recall, we both carried the ludicrous notion that being picked up by strangers in foreign countries would help us to learn the respective languages.

Shortly before we departed, Martin rang me with some good news. Some teaching colleagues of his (female colleagues, whoopee) would be willing to give us a lift all the way to France. I wasn't sure whether this fitted the purity of our venture, but it seemed an offer it would be foolish to refuse.

I certainly would have refused if I'd known that the girls' car was a 2CV. I had encountered these ramshackle creations all those years before in Tours, where the family I was staying with invited me to join them and their smelly baby for a picnic in the forest each Sunday. This was my introduction to the Meccano set which was a 2CV. Amazed to reach the forest alive, I was more amazed still to get home alive, in view of what happened in the forest.

Monsieur Moreau would park in a clearing, produce a spanner from the glove compartment, unbolt all the seats and remove them from the car for us to sit on. In fairness, this did make for exceptionally comfortable picnics, but it also meant that the seats were extensively stained with patches of tomato innards and smears of Camembert, while each crevice was packed with scratchy remnants of baguette.

That particular vintage of 2CV was the variety which was actually constructed out of corrugated iron. The one in which Martin and I joined Claudia and Petra was a much more modern affair, in fact brand new. Claudia rather nervously informed us that she hadn't actually driven it before, as she pulled out onto the *Autobahn* between two gigantic trailer-pulling juggernauts, both of which flashed and hooted at us threateningly. For a brief moment, I thanked my lucky stars that I was in the back seat, until I realised that Claudia's motorway driving style entailed getting into the outside lane at a low speed (a fully-laden 2CV is capable of no other speed) and ignoring any Mercedes, BMWs or lorries. These would come up behind us and hover a few millimetres away from the bean-can thin metal which was all that separated them from - well, from me.

The main feature of the early hours of the journey was thick fog. But nothing slows down German drivers. Liking to do everything just that little bit better than anyone else, they make sure that their motorway pile-ups involve more vehicles than those in any other country. Every few kilometres there would be vehicles on fire, people with their heads bandaged, dented cars and flashing ambulances. Not that this restrained Claudia in any way, as she continually held forth, gesticulating with one hand while maintaining only a tenuous connection between the other hand and the steering wheel.

The immense sensation of relief that I felt when we finally descended from the motorway was short-lived. This was because normal roads contain bends, and 2CVs were not designed to deal with bends, certainly not the way that Claudia threw herself into them. Had it been an Audi or something with some kind of advanced suspension system, maybe it would have been okay. But the 2CV had all the suspension of a perambulator without any of the stability.

If you travel as a passenger on the back of a motorbike (I don't recommend it, but there are those who thrive on it, mostly the wives of Hell's Angels), the first thing you are told is that, as you approach a bend, the driver will lean the machine over at an angle, and you will have to do the same. If you don't, you will seriously threaten the stability of the bike.

Well, I'm sorry, but I'm not going to do that. My natural instinct, surely not an unreasonable one, when seeing the ground rushing up towards me, is to move in the opposite direction. This means I normally refuse lifts on motorbikes, but I was unaware that the same principle applied to 2CVs. Every time Claudia hurled the tin can into a left-hand bend, the car would lean 45 degrees to the right, while I, in turn, would lean 45 degrees to the left. The same applied in reverse (i.e. when turning right), but I can't be bothered to describe that. As we came out of each bend, the car would then wobble about the road, usually into the path of some enormous vehicle approaching from the opposite direction.

Of course, I would scream. But Claudia said this was all my fault for not "going with the flow", rather than the fact that she was a shit driver. So the atmosphere in the 2CV soon became more than a little strained.

There was another reason for the icy vibe. Both Claudia and Petra were members of the KBW, or *Kommunistischer Bund Westdeutschlands*, a particularly po-faced, Soviet and IRA-supporting communist political party which had a strong presence in German schools. As far as I was concerned, despite being vaguely sympathetic towards the principles involved, this mainly meant that Claudia and Petra were boring and droned on about politics all the time. For Martin, it meant that he could pick good fights with them, and it wasn't long before I found it irresistible to join in.

We called them the "Well-Known Facts". This expression came from our avid listening to each Friday's edition of "Any Questions". Then, as now, there was invariably a preposterous Tory panelist who would claim, for example, that it was a "well-known fact" that foxes enjoyed being ripped to pieces by packs of hounds. Other favourite expressions of such opinion leaders are "any right-minded person" and "unacceptable", as in "any right-minded person" believes in the death penalty, and that any other view on the matter is "unacceptable"".

Well, sod off, Tory politician. I'll decide what is and isn't acceptable, thank you very much, and I will precede all my sweeping statements with "I think ..." It's not that much of a difference, I know, but that's why I just love it when Tony Benn makes some generalisation that I possibly don't agree with, and then disarmingly and charmingly adds, "Well, that's what I believe anyway, you can take it or leave it."

In perfect synergy with my (unoriginal) theory that extremes in politics form a full circle in that you can be so left-wing that you can end up being a fascist, Claudia and Petra were left-wing exponents of the "well-known fact" syndrome, i.e, my opinion isn't merely an opinion, it's a fact, and therefore there is no point in discussing it. When Martin and I would have the temerity to attempt to introduce a little light and shade into the proceedings, they would become apoplectic.

"We support the IRA because they are freedom fighters struggling against the Imperialist British."

"That's as may be, but do you support the IRA planting bombs?"

"Yes."

"But what if the bombs kill innocent people?"

"This is an unfortunate consequence of the struggle for freedom but justified by the eventual success of the campaign which will be for the good of all."

"Not for the good of the victims of the bombs."

"That is irrelevant."

"And what if one of your loved ones was inadvertently killed in a bomb blast?"

"That would be an acceptable consequence of the struggle."

"I don't believe you."

At such a point in the conversation, Petra would invariably get so frustrated that she would burst into tears. At KBW meetings, all the members would sit around agreeing with each other without the inconvenience of anyone questioning any of their Well-Known Facts. But Petra was famous for spending most of her waking hours crying. She would cry in the morning in fear of having to go to school and teach. Then she would cry during the lessons because the pupils ignored her. And finally, she would cry herself to sleep worrying about the next day. Martin and I developed a theory that the River Weser, into which the Pied Piper lured his rats, was formed entirely from the tears of Petra.

We developed one Well-Known Fact which genuinely was unshakably true, namely that all female KBW members were ugly, spotty and had short, greasy hair and thick spectacles as well as much facial hair and - oh God - excessive under-arm hair. This certainly held true for Petra and Claudia and for every other female KBW member we ever met, so obviously any Right Minded Person would agree with us. Oh, and they were all lesbians as well.

I say, let's hope nobody is leafing through this and taking it seriously.

In the evening, we arrived at Valenciennes, an uninviting industrial town in Northern France, where we planned to stay the night. Claudia drew the bean can up in front of an intimidatingly opulent-looking hotel and she and Petra disappeared into it. Speaking terms having long since been disconnected, we weren't invited to follow, so we didn't. The place looked far too snooty and expensive, so Martin and I walked a few yards to a *pension* round the corner and checked into an attic room which was so cheap that the landlady almost paid us to stay there.

In the morning, Petra and Claudia were furious, accusing us of abandoning them. In fact, they were just jealous that they had spent several hundred francs more than us for a probably not dissimilar night's sleep. An icy silence reigned until the time came for the parting of the ways just outside Paris. They wished us goodbye but not good luck. It was a Well-Known Fact, they said, that we wouldn't get any lifts because all drivers of anything other than 2CVs were capitalist pigs.

The first day's hitch through a bleak and unfriendly France contained many of the less attractive features of this unique mode of travel. For example, we had a series of brief lifts from village to village, distances so short that there was no progress at all to be discerned on the map. But these are lifts you can't really turn down. Invariably, the kind driver has screeched to a halt several hundred metres down the road (having had time to go through the "are they or are they not psychopaths?" thought process). As you run up to the car carrying your flapping belongings, the driver has kindly rearranged all the knick-knacks in the car in order to make space for you to sit. When the announcement is made that the driver is actually only travelling 3 km to the nearest hamlet, you can hardly be so ungrateful as to turn the lift down. So you don't. After all, it could have been a lift of hundreds of kilometres.

Then there is the inevitable unreasonable weather. In this case, it was snow, just outside Bordeaux. This led to our driver dropping us in a place called Marmande. We had thought that it wouldn't actually matter where we were dropped, in view of the fact that we didn't know where we were going, but Marmande was in such a cul-de-sac that we had no alternative but to hitch back the way we had come. Now that really was galling.

We entered the Basque Country and had coffee in Mont de Marsan. Now this pretty town is actually famous for a picturesque amphitheatre and numerous historical monuments, but for me, the only thing that mattered was that Mont de Marsan was to be the venue for a punk rock festival starring The Clash, The Damned and The Jam. Judging by the less than friendly looks we received, one can't imagine how the festival went. Well, actually, I know, because I've read numerous books on the subject. It was a catastrophe.

Our jerky progress took us on through Dax, Bayonne and St Jean de Luz, where we stayed the night in anticipation of an assault on Spain. This did not go well. In an attempt to reach San Sebastian, we were reduced to the worst ignominy a hitch-hiker can experience: catching a bus. Not one, but three buses.

The Rain In Spain falls mainly on San Sebastian, we discovered. And rain is not helpful to hitch-hikers. If you take shelter, you can't get lifts. But if you don't take shelter, you get drenched. And if you get drenched, drivers will show sympathy but decide in favour of the welfare of their upholstery. They will shrug their shoulders, pretend they have no room, or point sideways in a vain attempt to convince you that they will shortly be turning off. In San Sebastian, they did all of these things, all day. Or they ignored us. So we got wet. Then we got wetter, and indeed wetter. So we started to argue with each other.

Conversation while hitch-hiking is difficult. On the face of it, there's normally plenty to talk about, such as what bastards all the drivers flowing past are. But there is also plenty to disagree about, such as exactly where to stand, whether you are thumbing enthusiastically enough, whether it had been wise to accept the previous lift which plonked you in the middle of a 1950s housing estate, etc.

(Incidentally, we could easily have penned the authoritative Rough Guide to the 1950s Housing Estates of France and Spain - any offers?)

Sometimes, Martin and I had to stand for five or six hours in the same godforsaken spot. We initially had plenty of conversation topics, because we were both teaching in secondary schools and schoolteachers always have lots of things to discuss, moan and pontificate about. But eventually, silences would start to fall, and silences breed resentment. What is he thinking? That last remark seemed to suggest a criticism of my attitude, but if I question it, will I appear over-sensitive? And I don't agree with what he said anyway. He's annoying me. I'm probably annoying him. This is horrible.

We invented a few ways to fill the silences. These took the form of Radio 4 panel games, now long deceased, such as the Tennis Elbow Foot Game and Twenty Questions. The former was mainly uncontroversial, consisting of saying a word which had a connection with the previous word, without repeating any words or using unconnected ones. The challenges could be disputed, but it was normally relatively peaceful.

Twenty Questions, however, was far more challenging. For a start, one contestant had to pretend to be all four of the upper-crust panelists we remembered from our youth (I think Lady Isabel Barnett was one of them). And serious disagreements would break out:

"You said it was animal and vegetable but it's animal and mineral."

"No it isn't."

"Are you telling me that rubber is a vegetable?"

"Of course it is! They tap it out of trees. Anyway, you've had nineteen questions."

"No I haven't. I've only had eighteen. You shouldn't have charged me when I asked how many questions I'd had."

"Why not? It was a question."

To be fair, relations were normally pretty good, but not on that day we got stuck in San Sebastian. It was late afternoon before we eventually got picked up by two young men who tried to engage us in conversation about Basque separatism. Considering that our Spanish ran to *"Buenos dias"* and *"una cerveza"* and no further, this was a vain exercise, and they looked extremely annoyed when they dropped us only a few kilometres later. At that point, our luck changed, as we were picked up by a Uruguayan folk singer heading for Madrid. He took us all the way to Valladolid, an ugly city strongly reminiscent of Valenciennes and - spookily - sharing its initial syllable. Here we stayed the night in a horrible hotel and wished we had never left home.

In the morning, we decided we were fed up with Spain. The map said that it wasn't far to Portugal, so we thought we'd give that a whirl. After a while, until a man driving a taxi stopped for us. Now the last thing a hitcher wants to get involved with is a taxi, but the driver assured us that not only was he heading over the border into Portugal, but he was off duty and wouldn't charge us. As far as we could understand, he was telling us that he was so used to company that he couldn't bear to drive on his own. That's my type of taxi driver!

Sure enough, in return for us nodding, smiling and pretending we'd understood, he took us all the way to Mirandela, a pleasant river crossing town not far from the border, where we booked into the *Hotel Mira Tua*.

And that's why I wrote this book, because what happened there reflected all the most human and positive things about hitching and rough travelling. In the morning, Martin awoke to find he had serious food poisoning. Feeling worried, I fetched a doctor, who prescribed Martin some medicine and said he must stay in bed for a couple of days. Okay, we needed a bit of a rest, but I was frightened of catching whatever it was, and so spent the day wandering round the town.

Eventually, in the afternoon, I sat down in a town centre bar and ordered a coffee. In the corner sat a group of male youngsters who studied me intently. Uh-oh, I thought, trouble again, and made sure that, as in an aeroplane, I knew exactly where the exits were. Sure enough, after a few minutes, two of them approached me and addressed me in impeccable English:

"Are you from England?"

"Yes."

"Oh, do you like music?"

"Yes, I love music."(Their grins widened.)

"What is your favourite group?"

"I'm sure you don't know them. They're called Camel."

At this point, the grins almost went off the sides of their faces. Their friends came rushing over and animated conversation broke out.

"But this is wonderful. We have a band called Tribo and we play all Camel's songs."

Camel, for those 99 percent of you who don't know, was a seventies progressive rock band which specialised in lengthy organ and guitar instrumentals and rather pretentious concept albums. I shouldn't have liked them but I did and I still do. So this meeting was tremendously exciting.

Tribo immediately invited me to visit their rehearsal room that evening. The entire event seemed so bizarre that I was actually quite apprehensive about climbing into a van with a collection of total strangers and driving off into the dark hills. But their rehearsal room was a beautifully equipped barn and Tribo turned out to be my first-ever experience of the concept of a tribute band. Complete with a sound engineer and a light show, they performed a two-hour concert of note for note cover versions of Camel songs - just for me!

I should have kept a set list, but I'm certain they played the entire first album and much of the second. To show what a sad person I am, I noted down all the band's equipment and kept it for future reference. The future is now, so here's the list:

Farfisa organ, Fender Precision bass, Ludwig drum kit, Roland synthesiser, Solina mellotron, Fender Rhodes piano, Ibanez Stratocaster copy guitar, Italian LEM and British VOX amplification.

I'm so sorry, that was terribly boring.

Manuel Ceriz, Tribo's bassist, turned out to be the kindest person you could ever meet, and that is why we are still friends to this day. By the following morning, he had arranged for his old English teacher to give me a guided tour of the town, then invited me to have lunch with his family. I remember that they had loads of students from the outlying areas lodging with them, and that we all sat in the garden and sang songs. Many of the students were extremely beautiful girls who seemed interested in me, so the temptation to stay was strong, but Martin had recovered and we had agreed to head for the coast. But I will never forget Mirandela.

Manuel arranged for a timber lorry to take us from Mirandela to Porto. Kind though this was, it caused us considerable trauma, because this was a huge, open, articulated vehicle carrying enormous whole tree trunks. The road plunged along ravines, through forests and round hairpin bends, and the driver never took his foot off the accelerator once. Every now and then, we would thunder in and out of potholes so deep that I was convinced that at any second a tree trunk would blast through the back of the cab and take my head off. No, I will never forget Mirandela, and I will never forget that journey either.

On the map, we had picked out Viana do Castelo as a place which looked as if it would offer seaside and some rest. This turned out to be a quite beautiful town. Still adorned with symbolic communist murals, the narrow streets were shady and friendly, and we found a little hostel called *Impala*, which had a tiny balcony. As I stood on it to survey the scene, the shutters opened on the balcony opposite. The street was so narrow that one could almost (but not quite) have leaned across and touched it.

On the balcony stood four dark-haired, beautiful teenage girls, who blushed and giggled in a way which was seemingly inevitably inspired by the appearance of pale, dishevelled Englishmen. They were talking to me but of course I didn't know what they were saying.

"*Inglés?*" I offered, feebly.

"*Ah, Inglés!*"

One of the girls disappeared into the room and returned with a dictionary. After a moment's scrabbling, they agreed on the word they sought.

"*Whasssh?*"

"*Qué?*"

"*Whasssh ... momentito*" ... - scrabble, scrabble - "*you clozes?*"

"Christ," said Martin, "I think they're offering to wash our clothes."

I pointed to my shirt and made washing motions with my hands.

"*Si!*"

I picked up a sock and waved it in their direction, holding my nose.

"*Si!*"

This was amazing. I dug into my rucksack and pulled out a pair of dirty knickers. These, too, I waved at them, grimacing at their disgustingness.

"*Si, si!*"

How wonderful. As if as a mirror image of Petra and Claudia, these girls were as politically incorrect as you could imagine. We threw all our dirty clothes across the road, and within minutes they were dangling on a washing line from the balcony. I took a photo, on the assumption that this was something which would never occur again in my life. I was right.

This will never, ever happen again.

In the evening, the girls took us to an-out-of town disco, which involved a long walk across a road bridge which had the distinction of having been designed by Gustave Eiffel. Sadly, the disco was closed, but the following morning, the girls took us out again, this time up the funicular railway to the Church of Santa Lucia, a lovely building with spectacular views. I was in such a holiday mood that I even allowed a man with a box camera and a plastic parrot to take an expensive photo of us. Normally, I'd have scowled at such an offer.

The following day was a scenic hitch to Santiago de Compostela. Lifts included a cosmetics salesman and a Catholic priest. We had actually hoped to get much further, but found ourselves, late in the evening, in the cold and dark outside Santiago with no traffic around, and so had no alternative but to stagger into town. This was a stroke of luck, because, strange as it seems, considering how famous it is, I'd never heard of Santiago.We were instantly befriended by a gang of students who took us from bar to bar and disco to disco until we both ended up extremely pissed in the middle of the night. I regret to say that I remember little of the spiritual ambience of the town which attracts so many visitors; at least, not that kind of spirit.

Now, pay attention, because the next couple of paragraphs will give you an insight into the highs and lows of hitching. In the morning, we got a lift from a friendly communist, setting the pattern for the day's conversation in Pidgin Spanish: philosophy, religion and regional politics, all of them subjects on which I'd be normally hard-put to sustain a conversation in English. Martin's recommendation to simply add an -o to the end of every word wasn't particularly helpful. When I said *"I-o do-o nott-o believ-o in-o Godd-o"*, the driver didn't seem to understand at all. He dropped us in La Coruña and recommended us to head for Lugo, but in Lugo, we were dropped in an area where the roads clearly led - *à la* Talking Heads - to nowhere. So we had to walk three miles back into town and a further three miles back out the other side before finding a suitable slip road. This, with heavy rucksacks, was knackering.

We finally got picked up by someone who we understood to be

saying he was going sixty kilometres, but it turned out to be six. After another short lift with a wizened woodcutter, we had what seemed to be an amazing stroke of luck. A van driver picked us up, claiming to be going to Bilbao, which was just what we needed. We would get there at 4 am, he reckoned. At 12.30, we stopped at a transport café, and noticed that he was drinking heavily. Back in the van, he switched on some muzak at immense volume and, at 3.30 am, he suddenly announced that he was going no further and that we would have to get out.

The moment we had descended, he hurled our rucksacks into the road and accelerated away. Why he did this, I have no idea; maybe he thought that Martin and I were insulting him in some way as we nattered in English. It can, indeed, seem threatening when you don't understand what people are saying. Anyway, the result was that we were hopelessly stranded on a deserted country road from 3.30 am until 7.45 am, when we were finally rescued and taken to Santander. It goes without saying that the vibes were not good.

At lunch time, a miracle occurred. We were taken by an Italian honeymoon couple all the way to Bayonne in Southern France. This was a bit like the taxi driver conundrum: Why on earth would a honeymoon couple interrupt their blissful peace by inviting into their space a couple of smelly, bedraggled maniacs, when they could, like everyone else, have just driven past? It was incomprehensible, but we were grateful.

After a couple of sporadic lifts, we were then picked up by a fish lorry (which dripped salt water and scales out of the back), heading for Bordeaux. This was fine, and we intended to spend the night in a hotel which we spotted. The lorry had driven off before we discovered that the hotel was full. We dragged round town, but all the hotels were either full or shut. At about 1 am, we happened on a police station. I was so desperate and exhausted that I pressed a button on the intercom and explained our predicament. Was there any way they could help?

The intercom went dead. I pressed it again.

"Oui?"

"It's me again. Do you understand our problem?"

"*Oui.*"

"Can you help? Please?"

"*Non.*" Click.

Putain! Salope! Merde! - er - pity I was short on French swearwords, because those I knew weren't strong enough for what I felt about that particular *gendarme.*

At last, we got a lift to Poitiers, where we arrived at 4.30 am. At 6 am, a lorry took us to Tours, where we were sure there would be a hotel. *Mais non!* The *Office de Tourisme* informed us that, owing to a tobacco planters' conference in the town (a tobacco planters' conference!), all hotels were "*complet*". For goodness' sake! It had been 48 hours since we had last slept. It was 11 o'clock before we found a room, and we slept until evening.

The next day, our ways had to part. Martin was heading back to Germany, while I planned to visit my family in England and thus had to make for Le Havre. I decided to stay on in Tours for another day, exploring some old student haunts.

The evening threw up another unwelcome adventure. Innocently entering what I thought was a normal bar, I found myself approached by a not-unattractive lady who suggested I might like to buy her a drink. Oh, all right. It wasn't until I looked at the bill that I realised what sort of establishment I must have unwittingly entered. The beers cost 34 francs each! Of course, I had no such cash on me and had to choose my moment and "do a runner". Even thought I hadn't touched the drink, it was still terrifying, as I careered down a series of deserted streets until sure I wasn't being followed by a gun-toting pimp.

The following day, things were slightly better, because I was travelling alone. One driver was completely drunk (not all that unusual in France), and dumped me at what he insisted was a good spot: a three-lane motorway covered with signs saying "No Hitching". But luckily, a friendly Algerian, charging up the outside lane, screeched through three lanes of enraged truckers, picked me up and took me all the way to the ferry port.

Phew. I'll never hitch again. Will I?

Chapter 4.

Hitch-hiker's Guide To Lunacy

Will I? Only a madman would have considered setting off on another hitch-hiking holiday. And so I did.

In fact, I did retain quite pleasant memories of the previous summer's debacle, although, apart from Mirandela, it would be a challenge to remember what they were. But this time, the circumstances were completely different. For a start, I was on my own. Secondly, it was Easter. Thirdly, I had, in the meantime, fallen in love and didn't actually want to be anywhere other than with my loved one. And lastly, it was a bet.

A bet? If there's any justice, this book will now become a best-seller, just like that one about a bloke hitching round Ireland with a fridge. Yes, for a bet, I hitched from North Germany to Italy and back to Denmark in the space of ten days.

Originally, it was just going to be a trip to Italy, but in the period between planning this and executing it, my relationship with Birgit had begun. She announced that she had quite different plans for the Easter holidays. She would be going to visit friends in Copenhagen. It was while bemoaning to Martin the fact that Birgit and I had only just got together and were now heading off in diametrically opposite directions, that he sowed the idea:

"Why don't you hitch to Copenhagen instead?"

"But I've already made arrangements to stay with friends on the way south."

"Okay, why don't you hitch to Copenhagen as well?"

"As well? Are you mad? I'd never make it."

"Bet you could."

"Bet I couldn't."

"How much?"

"Fifty marks."

"Done."

It was only after the conclusion of the deal that I realised that the bet was a pretty damn topsy-turvey affair. The only way that I could triumph, i.e. achieve what I was setting out to achieve, would be to lose the bet. After all, I was the one who was claiming that it couldn't be done, but I was also the one who then set out, with some determination, to prove that indeed it could. Story of my life.

I didn't tell Birgit that I intended to join her in Denmark, in case I didn't make it. Plus, I liked the idea of a dramatic and romantic unexpected arrival. So, after a fond farewell, I donned my trusty orange rucksack and commenced the journey south with the same lift with which I always left Bremen: an offer I should have refused, but didn't, all the way to the Wildeshausen Services, a mere fifteen or so kilometres down the motorway. Italy, let alone Copenhagen, suddenly seemed an awful long way away. Still, to look on the bright side, at least if I didn't make it, I'd end up fifty marks better off.

Münster, about 200 kilometres south of Bremen, was the university town where I'd arranged my first stop, with some old student friends from Kiel. One of the great things about university studies in Germany is that you can do the odd year here and the odd year there, according to where you feel like being, and it all counts towards your degree. This particular bunch had got fed up with Kiel and decided that Münster would be more fun.

When I got to Münster, I realised that, among this group of friends, there had been a startling change of relationships and atmosphere. It appeared that Jens had stolen Peter's girlfriend. Peter had reacted very badly. He and Jens were no longer on speaking terms and Peter, to work out his frustration, had thrown himself into the unsavoury activity of bodybuilding, a topic about which he could talk endlessly (and very boringly). As for my closest friend Hartmut, he had changed completely in the year or so since I'd last seen him. Far from being the jolly, lazy student type I remembered, he had decided to start working seriously for his degree. What was worse, he had changed subjects from Law to Religion, in which the University of Münster specialised.

I had been looking forward to going out with my friends to Münster's famously riotous student quarter. After I had dropped the hint a few times, Hartmut and I set off. We sat in a corner of a *"Studentenlokal"* and I tried to recall Old Times, but Hartmut insisted on putting a Christian slant on everything. Heretically, he said he now regretted and felt embarrassed about half the things I remembered with such pleasure.

At about 10 pm, the door burst open and in came Peter, covered with sweat from an intense workout in the gym which he had started four hours previously. Illogically (if good health was his purpose), he started drinking heavily. Obviously, good health was not his motivation; he was working out and boozing in order to forget his troubles. Unfortunately, his troubles were following.

Quite by chance (or maybe not), who should then enter the pub but Jens, with Peter's ex-girlfriend on his arm. Peter, under the influence of the lethal schnapps, had been getting steadily more obnoxious, and I feared a major Western-style brawl complete with much hurling of tables and breaking of chairs over heads. But instead, Peter simply burst into tears. Uncontrollable floods of tears, complete with heaving sobs. Jens and his girlfriend had the temerity to sit a couple of tables away from us, pretending they hadn't noticed Peter (which they had).

Hartmut was sanctimoniously unsympathetic, declaring that Peter's condition was his own fault for drinking too much (and rubbing salt into the wound by implying that this was the reason that he had been left in the first place). I felt more inclined to take Peter's side; after all, I had recently fallen in love and was already missing Birgit something rotten. So I put my arm round Peter's shoulders and said something along the lines of "There, there". In fact, I may very well have said "Da Da Da", thus anticipating a Number One hit by Trio by several years. I ended up carrying Peter home.

In the morning, I had intended hitching onwards, but allowed myself to be persuaded by Peter, as part of his ongoing health régime, to accompany him to the sauna. Just why I allowed this to happen, I don't know. I have always thought that the sauna is a stupid concept. Why? Well, listen.

When I was young, my mother would always say, "If you're going out into the cold, make sure you wrap up well, otherwise you'll catch your death of cold." Your mother said that too, didn't she? All mothers say that, and all mothers are right. Every time I disobeyed her, I caught my death of cold. And now, every time our own children disobey us in this manner, they catch their death of cold too. Serve them right.

It therefore follows that saunas, far from being incredibly healthy, as their users claim, are, if fact, bad for you. If going from a centrally heated house into a rainstorm gives you a cold, then what, pray, is the natural consequence of heating your body up to a temperature far higher than it was designed to cope with, and then plunging it into a bath of icy water far colder than it was designed to cope with? Eh? And then going back and starting again. It's madness.

Peter poo-pooed my reservations as the ramblings of someone with no understanding of good health and insisted that I should come with him. And that's another thing. While you're in there torturing yourself (nobody can tell me this is a pleasure), so are loads of other people, all of them - at least in Germany - stark naked. It would be quite nice if all of them were pert-breasted nubile young girls, but on this occasion (and I admit that it's an experience I've never repeated), everyone was saggy-chested and droopy-willied. I didn't at all want to to look at their horrible bodies, but that's because I'm British and old-fashioned (so they tell me). And, although admittedly Peter was in reasonable shape, I didn't want to look at him either, in case he got the wrong idea. There was nothing else to look at apart from dripping walls and pine slats, and a newspaper would simply have disintegrated, so I just fixed my eyes on the middle distance and prayed for a swift release.

The moral of this story is that, of course, dear Mother was quite correct. Within minutes of leaving the sauna, I was sneezing violently and had to continue my journey south pouring phlegm into packet after packet of tissues, which naturally upset many of my lift-givers.

I suppose lots of people change in their mid-twenties; it's when life tends to start in earnest. Scarcely recovered from the crises of Hartmut and Peter, my next stop (lifts being plentiful and quick, some of them hurtling down the Autobahn in plushy, leather-upholstered Mercedes driven by businessmen) was with an old student friend from England called Mark, now residing in the Rhineland.

I remembered Mark as a mad, humorous, irresponsible piss-artist with whom I had shared accommodation in conditions of cheerful squalor. I looked forward with certainty to going out drinking and having a generally raucous time. But Mark's circumstances had changed in two crucial ways. First, he had got a job as a schoolteacher. Well, okay, so had I, but Mark was teaching at the only school in a small town in an area notorious for its conservatism. And secondly, oh dear, Mark had got married. His wife was a painfully quiet, conventional and respectable lady and was obviously, in the manner of how you imagine a German "*Hausfrau*", intensely houseproud. The moment I entered the flat, I got the message as to how dramatically Mark's lifestyle had changed. All the furniture was pristine, brand-new Scandinavian pine, every inch of shelf space was taken up with knick-knacks and house plants, and of dust there was not the slightest hint.

As with Hartmut, all my sentences beginning, "Cor, do you remember the time when ...?" were greeted with responses which indicated, yes, well, we were young then, but we're adults now, aren't we? And by the way, what on earth are you doing hitch-hiking at your age?

In Germany, they stagger their school holidays, which meant that, although mine had started, Mark still had to teach at 7.30 the next morning, even though it was a Saturday. So we spent our Friday evening in a way slightly different from what I had planned. We stayed in, drank coffee and orange juice and played Scrabble. They doubtless believed that they had the perfect lifestyle, but it was not one to which I aspired.

The next stop was Würzburg, and the people I was spongeing off this time were Chris, another teacher from Bremen, and his girlfriend Effi, who was studying in Würzburg. Chris had offered me a lift down in his car, but remember the bet? No, thought not. I had to hitch everywhere, remember? I suppose I could have arranged to position myself, thumb aloft, somewhere near Chris's flat on the day he left, but that would have been cheating and that would have been out of the question. Besides, he knew Martin, and might have snitched.

Chris and Effi had the kind of relationship which people call "volatile". They were forever splitting up and getting together again. You know the kind of couples who have screaming, violent rows, throwing vases at each other, scratching each other with their finger nails and pulling each other's hair, before finally falling into each other's arms and making passionate love on the kitchen floor? Maybe quite exciting, actually, but probably not in the long term. Anyway, Chris and Effi were such a couple.

Sadly, my arrival coincided with the aftermath of a major bust-up. The plan had been for them to spend the evening showing me round this beautiful and historic town, but the circumstances were not at all what I had anticipated. At any given time, either Chris would walk, shoulders hunched in an attitude of terminal doom, a few paces ahead of us while Effi explained to me in detail just what a shit Chris was. Or else, Effi would walk ahead, unsuccessfully pretending not to care, while Chris told me what a cow she was. In both cases, I framed non-committal replies along the lines of:

"Yes, of course I see what you're saying, but on the other hand there may be another side to the story, and I'm sure it will all work out in the end."

They didn't like that at all. They wanted me to take sides. Anyway, I didn't learn much about the architectural merits of Würzburg, and in the evening, Effi announced that she was going to stay the night with a girlfriend. When I woke up in the morning, Chris had disappeared, presumably in pursuit of his loved / hated one. Quite possibly, they were making passionate love on the kitchen floor at that very moment. Bastards!

I moved on, leaving them to their own devices. When I next met

Chris, he acted as if nothing had happened. Apparently this had been but a minor blip in their relationship.

In order to win / lose the bet, I had to crack on, so crack on I did. Good lifts continued, through Munich, up into the Alps and eventually into Innsbruck. Now this place always looks lovely in TV ski shows, but I remember it as being austere, grey and overpowering. Running short of cash, I booked myself into the Youth Hostel.

Depressing places at the best of times, this particular Youth Hostel took the biscuit. The dormitory I was in housed the usual selection of misfits: an elderly hiker, a couple of backpackers and a group of giggling schoolboys. I remember this hideous night in all its horrible detail.

For a start, it was lights out at 10.30, silence at 11 o'clock. The hiker and the backpackers respected this, but they had problems of their own. The backpackers had taken off their copious socks and the stink of their feet was unbelievable. Pungent fumes of prime Gorgonzola wafted up my nose and induced a state of nausea, making sleep an impossibility. But it would have been an impossibility anyway, because the elderly hiker had a severe snoring problem.

And snoring is a problem, isn't it? Maybe if it was a regular thing, you could force yourself to grow accustomed to it, rather like with a ticking alarm clock. But this man's snoring was interspersed with grunts, splutters, sighs, shouts and, most unnervingly, orgasmic sighs. At one stage, I actually got up and prodded him, but he didn't even notice.

The backpackers slept on, presumably anaesthetised by their own socks. But the worst hindrance to sleep was the group of boys. At 11 o'clock, a loud tannoy announcement (tough luck if you'd already dropped off) told us that silence must now reign. For a moment, it did, until one of them farted. That started off a hail of hysterical laughter which seemed to go on for at least ten minutes, despite the shushings of both me and the old hiker who (small mercies) had been woken by the commotion.

Eventually, everything calmed down, but not for long. Go on, cast your mind back and admit it: If you'd been there and you'd been fourteen, you, too, would have concentrated your mind on brewing up the most spectacularly loud fart in history. In due course, it exploded, closely followed by three or four more from other competitors who had just failed to win the race. That was it. They all rolled around the floor, clutching their stomachs and screeching. It was so noisy that even the backpackers woke up, perhaps sensing in these new noxious gases some unfair competition for their own aromas.

There was only one solution. I pulled my mattress from the bunk, dragged it out through the door and found a few hours' fitful sleep in the brightly lit corridor outside. My feelings towards the hostel warden who switched on a deafening tape of Austrian brass band music at 6.30 a.m. would not be possible to put into words.

Things were getting more and more urgent, since I had to get over the Alps and into Italy in order to send the postcard which would prove that I had made it. A series of short lifts took me to Bolzano, the first town over the Italian border. It seemed a nondescript sort of place. It was raining and there was no one about at all. I checked into some sort of hostel but was intimidated by my poor understanding of Italian - did I even have enough money to pay the bill? To make sure, I had a packet of crisps instead of supper.

I was the only person in the building. Even the grumpy woman who had let me in seemed to have left, and I was in a tiny, dingy attic room. Everything was dismal and grey, and I found myself falling into a deep depression. What the hell was I doing here? I had just fallen hopelessly in love for the first and only time in my life, and the object of my affections was about as far away as it was possible to be while still remaining in Europe. Or so it seemed. What was more, I had entered this predicament voluntarily.

There was nothing for it. I'd have to write some poems. Considering that I've always hated poetry, this was an odd decision, but now I was beginning to attain an insight into the kind of agonising heartache which makes people put pen to paper in this way. I am a hoarder, so somewhere in my house, the poems I composed in the garret in Bolzano must still exist. I have never looked for them, because I am sure they are a load of pretentious, self-pitying old crap.

It must have been a cathartic action, though, because, in the morning, I felt more positive about the impending journey to Scandinavia. After all, that was where Birgit was, and if I wanted to see her, I had better damn well get there. So, in the continuing rain, I made my way to the edge of Bolzano and stuck out my thumb.

I remember a feeling of great joy when, almost immediately, a young man stopped and wound down his window. Great music boomed from his stereo and he grinned in a welcoming way. But he only spoke Italian. By a mixture of gesticulating, pointing and saying "Garmisch-Partenkirchen" in what I thought was an Italian accent, I convinced myself that he was going all the way to this distant ski resort which lay precisely on my planned route. It was perfect! With a light heart, I climbed in.

He drove two exits into the forest, a distance of about five kilometres, turned off the main road and stopped. I honestly don't think he meant any harm; he had probably been saying he was going in the **direction** of Garmisch-Partenkirchen. At any event, he dropped me in the worst place that my extensive hitching career had ever experienced, on a totally deserted slip road in the midle of a dark forest.

The only traffic was the occasional timber lorry, obviously on a short haul (and ignoring me anyway). Somewhere within earshot, a group of foresters was working in the woods. They were yodelling. I promise it's true. They were yodelling, I tell you. Which was probably quite funny, but I didn't find it amusing at all.

Every so often, while hitching, something happens which you assume must be a mirage. After I had been waiting for a good five hours, I started to think the unthinkable and contemplate walking back to Bolzano and recommencing my - this time probably suicidal - poetry writing. But out of the shadows suddenly appeared an ancient little brown Daf, one of those tiny cars which looked almost like a toy.

"Garmisch-Patenkirchen?" I enquired.

"Dunno. Is that in goddam Italy, goddam Austria or goddam Germany?" asked the car's male occupant.

"Oh, you're American."

"Sure I am. Can you get me out of this goddam place?"

"Where are you going?"

"Frankfurt."

"Frankfurt," I gulped. "You don't mean Frankfurt am Main?"

"Yes sir, I sure do."

This definitely had to be a deranged mirage, brought on by prolonged exposure to yodelling. Frankfurt was several hundred kilometres away in central Germany. I'd have normally expected to take two days to get there.

"Let's get this straight. You're an American, you're lost and you want me to direct you to Frankfurt?"

"That's about the size of it."

The alacrity with which I attempted to hurl my rucksack into the car was only slightly dampened by the fact that the back seat was so small that it hardly fitted. But it didn't matter. I was on my way to Frankfurt!

Joe was a sergeant in the US army, stationed near Frankfurt. Just why he'd driven to Italy he was coy about, but he was full of opinions, mainly about how much he hated the goddam Italians, the goddam Austrians and, above all, the goddam Germans. Any feelings he might have had about the goddam Brits he mercifully kept to himself.

Apart from the cramped conditions and the necessity to nod enthusiastically in agreement with Joe's increasingly fascist pronouncements, everything went swimmingly. We stopped for coffee in the legendary Garmisch-Patenkirchen. Ironically, we had already descended from the Alps when something completely unexpected happened, considering it was Easter time. It started to snow.

"Goddam, what the hell is that?" asked Joe.

"It's snow, Joe," I replied, resisting the temptation to add, "but not as we know it."

The problem was, of course, that Joe didn't know it. Coming from Tucson, Arizona, his only prior knowledge of this meteorological phenomenon was seeing it lying quietly on the Alpine peaks we had just passed. That it actually came from the sky and settled on roads he hadn't contemplated.

At first, it was all quite jolly, because Joe was entranced. But before long, it developed into a situation which posed severe danger to both of us, not to mention the other users of the motorway. All the other vehicles (of which there were plenty, mainly heavy lorries) pulled onto the hard shoulder and either stayed there or fitted chains before they carried on. But Joe, determined to get to Frankfurt, was having none of this lily-livered goddam German caution and kept his foot pressed firmly to the floor.

This was actually probably inadvertently the best policy, because any application of the brakes would have sent the tiny, light vehicle into a spin, probably into the path of one of the lorries. Whatever, I was one hundred percent convinced that we were guaranteed to have an accident sooner or later.

It actually happened later, just outside the town of Ulm. It was pitch dark and the wipers suddenly stopped working. I don't think they broke down, they just got overwhelmed by the force of the blizzard. The sudden loss of vision unnerved Joe sufficiently to make him apply the brakes and off we went, round and round in circles, somehow weaving in and out of the lorries. We thundered into the central reservation, bounced off it, hurtled across two lanes and disappeared down the embankment into a field.

Obviously, we were dead. Except that we weren't. The one thing the car hadn't done was turn over, so we were both still there, sitting upright and looking at each other as if nothing had happened. I cautiously opened the door and was amazed to see lights, just a couple of hundred metres away across the field. What was more, the lights appeared to be moving. It seemed that we were near a road, so we struggled towards it. From the signs, it looked as if it was the road into Ulm, so off we set along it. All attempts at flagging down cars failed; we must have looked pretty scary. Poor Joe, clearly traumatised, had no thought of calling out the recovery services.

In fact, he was now not at all the macho all-American soldier, and I almost had to carry him.

"Find me a hotel, find me a hotel," he kept pleading, not realising that I was in no better position to locate a hotel than he was. But in the town centre, we found one, and Joe disappeared into it. That was it. I couldn't have afforded the hotel, so had to set out in search of the Youth Hostel, which turned out to be at the top of a long, steep hill. As the snow was now a foot deep and my footwear, as usual, totally unsuitable, I suffered the indignity of having to ascend it on all fours. With my orange rucksack on my back I must have resembled a demented psychedelic tortoise.

I got to the youth hostel just in time for the spartan supper, which I recall consisted of bread and cheese spread. And the bastards made me wash up. There is a German tongue twister which goes "*In Ulm, um Ulm, um Ulm herum*". Although I can't say it with any ease, I know precisely what it means: "In Ulm, round Ulm, round about Ulm". Yeah, they're playing my song.

On the way back up through Germany, I stayed with all the people I'd stayed with on the way down. Chris and Effi were reconciled and seemed to resent my invasion of their love nest. Mark and his wife again showed no interest in going out to the pub and Peter was offended when I refused to accompany him to the sauna.

I eventually found myself in Eckernförde, in Schleswig-Holstein, but a throw of a stone from my destination. The Youth Hostel was full and refused to admit me. I had thought that they had to find somewhere for you if you were a member, but apparently not. I ended up sleeping on the beach, knocked out by half a bottle of rum.

In Eckernförde, an event occurred that was even madder than everything else that had happened on the journey. Passing what appeared to be a normal pub late at night, I heard, coming from inside, what seemed to be a couple having an energetic sex session.

But there was something odd about it. Not only did the sound effects seem to have been crudely amplified (including crackles and feedback) but the noises sounded like the soundtrack to a porn film (i.e. not genuine).

"*Oh ja, ja, oh ja, ja, ja,*" screamed the woman.

"*Mensch, bist du geil,*" replied the man, grunting.

"*Mehr, mehr, oh, oh, ich komme,*" added the woman, unconvincingly. (By the way, I won't be offended if this passage is entered for the Bad Sex Awards.)

Intrigued (go on, who wouldn't be?), I upended a handy beer crate and peered through the window. Sure enough, there on the little stage was a couple simulating sex. In the time-honoured tradition, she had pneumatic breasts and he sported a dark gringo moustache and a medallion. It was horrible but, of course, fascinating too.

"*Hey Sie,*" came an angry voice from behind me. "*Was machen Sie da?*"

Well, he had a point. I should really have paid twenty marks to get in and ten marks for each drink. Not for the first time and not for the last, I scarpered down a dark alleyway.

Setting out the following morning. I found another guy hitching where I wanted to be, so we agreed to team up. Called Klaus, he was a German student from Berlin, and we got on great. Just as well, in view of what was to happen.

After a while, we were picked up by a sallow-skinned, frightening-looking individual in an ancient VW Beetle. You know how it is when you meet someone and instantly register trouble? That's how we both felt, but of course, you don't turn down lifts. Having ascertained, firstly, that the man spoke no German, and secondly, that he was heading for the Puttgarten ferry to Denmark, where we wanted to go, we climbed in. But it soon became clear that this was to be no ordinary journey. The main problem was that the brakes on the VW weren't working. Every time we approached a junction or a traffic light, the driver simply pulled on the handbrake and screeched to a halt. This was worrying, as were the vaguely threatening remarks he kept making.

As we drew into the ferry port, our host turned to us:

"Now you give money for ferry."

"But we haven't got enough money to pay for the car."

"You find money," - at this point, he drew a knife from his pocket - "or you walk with your feets."

With some courage, my new friend Klaus, who was sitting in the front, grabbed the driver's wrist and squeezed until the knife was dropped. As the driver scrabbled on the floor in an effort to retrieve the knife, we two hitchers threw ourselves out of the door and ran like the wind. As we reached the ferry terminal, a police car was pulling up alongside the VW. Presumably he was wanted for something, at the very least dangerous driving.

When I arrived in Copenhagen, having both won and lost my bet, and eager for a fond reunion with Birgit, I had forgotten one thing: During the course of the journey, I had scarcely had an opportunity to shave and had therefore grown quite a significant beard. As I arrived at the door of the flat where Birgit was staying, she emerged and walked straight past me.

She only didn't bloody recognise me, that's all.

Chapter 5.

I Am A Doughnut

I may well be the only person in the world who wishes that the Berlin Wall had never come down. True, from any political or humanitarian point of view, this is an untenable attitude, but it's also undeniable that, for the tourist, Berlin is now a less exciting city than it used to be.

My first ever visit to Berlin was to set the tone for all subsequent ones. It was tense, dark, cold, intimidating, yet at the same time thrilling. I was a young student and became involved with a gang of people who worked at night, fly-posting for a travel company. Armed with extremely messy buckets of flour and water paste and enormous paintbrushes, we were transported in a van on a tour of building sites, all of them clearly marked with signs forbidding bill posting. It was January, when Berlin is at its bone-crunching coldest. And we were in permanent fear of arrest, having, on several occasions, to scatter and flee from the police down cobbled side streets. Okay, so maybe bill posting wasn't quite in the league of inter-state espionage, but it did feel a wee bit like something out of a Len Deighton novel.

For some reason, it was again in the depths of winter when, in 1970, some German friends and I set out from Kiel to Berlin, five of us crammed into a very uncomfortable VW Beetle. We negotiated the border controls at Helmstedt and embarked on the spooky trip through East Germany, during which you were not allowed to stop or to deviate from the deeply pot-holed motorway. It was dark and slightly confusing as we reached the crucial junction where you either headed into West Berlin or off into the wilderness of the DDR, eventually ending up in East Berlin (which, of course, you were not allowed to do). The trick (which we didn't know) was to watch out for signs saying *Berlin-West* and to ignore any saying *Berlin - Hauptstadt der DDR*. I'm pretty sure it was my fault that we took the wrong one. The windows were misted over and I think I just saw a sign saying something about Berlin and directed the driver that way.

Before long, we became aware that there was suddenly no traffic around any more. And, shortly after that, that a strange rumbling sound was emitting from beneath the Beetle, which was driving along at a bit of a strange angle. We had had a puncture.The second we pulled onto the hard shoulder and stopped, the DDR police were with us, unfriendly and threatening, as if they genuinely thought we could be spies (a laughable concept). Did we realise that we were trespassing without permission in a foreign country and that the penalties would be severe?

No excuses or explanations cut any ice at all with these automatons. Even in the dark, even a foreign person should be able to tell the difference between *Berlin-West* and *Berlin - Hauptstadt der DDR*. It was clear that we were there on purpose and up to some unspecified no good. Eventually, they agreed to lead us back to the correct highway in return for the statutory fine. But first, there was the little matter of the flat tyre. The policemen retired to their patrol car and watched as we struggled with iced fingers to undo the rusted bolts and replace the wheel, accompanied by many curses, insults and recriminations.

When this operation had finally been completed, we were led off on what we were later told was standard procedure: a seemingly pointless wild goose chase round the DDR countryside, designed, in fact, to empty our tank of petrol. The policemen made us follow them for what seemed like several hours down all sorts of country lanes and through dark forests until they drove onto the forecourt of a petrol station, where we contributed to the East German economy by filling up with their petrol. Having driven such an enormous distance, we couldn't even protest that we didn't need any.

Back on the correct Autobahn, we finally arrived at our destination, which was, I can't remember why, a nurses' home in a clinic on the outskirts of the city, where someone had lent us a room to stay in. Sadly, it being the middle of the night, the building was locked, so we crashed out in the car park. Five adults in a Beetle are cosy but not comfortable, so sleep was fitful, to put it kindly. Every bone in our bodies ached, and of course it was below freezing as well.

As dawn broke, we were awoken by an angry doctor, whose private parking space we had unwittingly taken, tapping on the window. Loads of attractive nurses were streaming into work and staring at us curiously. Sadly, attractive was not an adjective which could have been applied to us, because we were pale, unshaven, ill-looking and yet inevitably puffing on our first cigarette of the day before we were even properly awake. The medical passers-by must surely have been confident that they had spotted some future candidates for treatment.

Breakfast in Berlin

Later in the day, we decided to enter East Berlin legitimately. There were convoluted rules on how to go about this. If you were a resident of West Berlin, you weren't allowed in at all, because West Berlin wasn't recognised as legitimate. If you were any other West German citizen, you could visit, as could people from other countries, but you had to use different transit points. So, effectively, I entered East Berlin on my own.

For a person of my relatively young years, the procedure was very intimidating. Descending from the S-Bahn at Friedrichstrasse, you then entered a long series of dank, grey tunnels until you came to a row of steel-doored cubicles, like tiny cells. When your turn came to enter one of these, you had to stand in it until, suddenly, a flap about the size of a letter box would clank open and you would be confronted by a pair of cold, steely eyes staring straight into yours. A brief interrogation would then take place, accompanied by a minute inspection of the passport and a seeming pore by pore, eyelash by eyelash examination of the passport photo. This was of particular interest in my case, on account of the fact that the photo showed a fresh-faced, short-haired freckly schoolboy, while the reality was an exhausted, unhealthy-looking stubbly adult apparition.

Before you were allowed onto East Berlin soil, you had to change five marks into DDR currency at the rate of one *"West-Mark"* to one *"Ost-Mark"*. This didn't seem like much money, but such was the gigantic disparity between the two currencies that it was virtually impossible to spend the money in the East, no matter how hard you tried. Plus, there was absolutely nothing in the shops that anyone would want to buy.

We travelled around the city a bit on the trams, but not even that was a good way to spend money. Using a method which I still believe to be the finest example ever of how to run a public transport system, the East Berlin trams operated on an Honesty principle. Each carriage contained a loo-roll of raffle tickets on a string. You took your ticket and, if you felt like it, you inserted some kind of coin into a thing like a little wooden church donation box. Anxious to conform, we watched to see if anyone would put any money into it. Nobody did, so we didn't either. Unsurprisingly, all the trams were packed with grateful passengers.

I spent some time in a bookshop near the Alexanderplatz. This emporium specialised in books for teaching German to foreigners, all of them tailored to the world view which was compulsory in Communist Eastern Europe: These artefacts were so fascinating and potentially useful for my language coaching activities that I took several of them to the checkout, where I discovered that I had managed to exceed my allotted five marks. Never mind, said the kind assistant, we accept West-marks as well. So, with no further thoughts at all, I handed over the difference in Western money.

In the evening, we went in search of some bright lights in the form of an East Berlin discothèque. Having travelled a great distance into the suburbs, we were treated to a stilted evening in what amounted to a youth club, with wooden benches, soft drinks only, virtually no girls and uninterrupted *"Volksmusik"* (because, of course, Western pop was *verboten* on account of being decadent).

I knew that I had to be back at Friedrichstrasse by midnight because I had only been issued with the standard 24-hour visa, which expired at 12 o'clock. Arriving back in the steel cubicle with the eye-level letter box, I felt reasonably sure that no incident involving pumpkins and glass slippers would occur, and that the procedure for getting out wouldn't be too much worse than the one for getting in. But I had reckoned without the politically-correct teaching matter in my bag.

The officials did their sums and noticed the discrepancy. How had I managed to buy seven marks' worth of books if I had only exchanged five marks? Because I had paid the rest in West-marks. Oh yes? We don't think so, because, if you had, it would have been marked as such on the receipt, and it wasn't. I had quite clearly been changing money on the black market, which was, as they were sure I was aware, a very serious crime indeed.

I was dumbfounded. Heck, it was only 24 hours since the last time I had completely innocently stumbled into a situation in which I was regarded as a criminal. All I could think of suggesting was that I could go back to the bookshop and claim the correct receipt. But it was way past shop-closing time, so there was no choice, they said, other than to detain me overnight. Feeling extremely frightened after a long and aggressive interrogation, large parts of which I hadn't been able to understand, I slept intermittently under a smelly blanket in a small, cold, grey cell, accompanied by a young oriental-looking man who spoke neither German nor English.

In the morning, in the company of a monosyllabic official, I was allowed to return to the bookshop, where - phew - the assistant recognised and remembered me. The correct receipt was issued and I was free to find my way back to the nurses' home and my worried friends, who had been more than a little concerned about my welfare. I spent most of the day asleep.

Starting to leaf through *"Deutsch - Ein Lehrbuch für Ausländer"*, the exciting book which had nearly got me locked up for life, I realised that it said a great deal about the world view in Eastern Germany. Here is an example of the kind of passage it contained:

"Foreign journalists are often surprised about the status of women in the DDR. They are very interested in Equality For Women, and therefore often ask questions about it. You can find women in almost any profession. Over 70 percent of women between the ages of 16 and 60 are in work. For example, about 40 percent of building workers and about 70 percent of health workers are women. Of course, they receive the same salary as men for their work. Working women don't have an easy life, because they also have to do the housework. The men help them, and the State has introduced a number of measures to make life easier, for example Kindergartens, and a system whereby the housewife hands in a shopping list at the factory gate at the start of her working day, and can collect the groceries when she leaves."

That was the glory of Communism. It all made such perfect sense, it was all so reasonable. Unfortunately, in practice, it was also largely a pack of lies.

Back in West Berlin, I began to have a vague (and naturally unfulfilled) notion of doing some research into ideologically contrasting methods of German teaching, and so set out in search of a Western equivalent of *"Deutsch - Ein Lehrbuch für Ausländer"*. I soon found *"Heute Abend"*, which displayed a view of Women's Equality somewhat different from its DDR companion:

Translate into German:

"How are you, Mrs. Miller?"

"Quite well, thank you. And how are you?"

"Very well, thank you, but I have a lot to do. Spring is a terrible time for us housewives, isn't it ?"

"Yes, you're right. The men don't know what it's like. I hardly have time to cook these days, and my husband complains, but I can't help that."

"Are you papering your rooms again this spring?"

"No, not this year. Are you?"

"Yes, I am papering the sitting-room. I bought a beautiful light-blue paper last week. I always think a paper looks nice in the sitting-room. But the other rooms I only distemper."

"Are you doing it yourself?"

"No, I can't do it; I have a man from the shop who does it for me. He papers and distempers very well."

"Is he very dear?"

"He's not cheap, but I said to my husband, I must have him, I can't do it alone."

The last evening was spent in what must be the oddest pub in Europe, with the possible exception of O'Donahue's bar in Dublin. Leydicke still exists, but back then, it was still run by "Mutter Leydicke", the aged and eccentric owner, who by then was well into her nineties. This place was the ultimate student haunt, so full that in order to get a drink, you had to give your money and your order to the person nearest you and watch it as it was passed from hand to hand to the bar, and then watch again as the drink gradually wended its way back to you. This is a system which also operates in O'Donahue's.

What was particularly odd about Leydicke was the nature of the drinks. The only thing they sold was their own home-made wine, which they manufactured out of unlikely and deadly combinations of fruits. The best one to order, I was assured, was the speciality of the house: *Stachelbeerwein*, or gooseberry wine.

Everybody has their own "I've never been as pissed as ..." story, and this is mine. So severe was the intoxication inflicted on me by my ribald friends' plying me with *Stachelbeerwein* (it wasn't my fault, obviously), that I myself can't remember anything of the events which allegedly occurred. As we left the pub, I failed to notice that there was a large hole in the road where it was being repaired, and thus tumbled head first into it. Unwilling to put in the effort required to climb out again, and anaesthetised by gooseberries against the sub-zero temperatures, I announced my intention of sleeping there. It apparently took several people to drag me out.

This appalling behaviour continued back at the nurses' home. In fact, come to think of it, that weekend consisted mainly of being arrested for things I shouldn't have been arrested for, whilst not being arrested for things I should have been arrested for. It is said that I spent the night charging round the building hammering on doors and yelling in English, "Where are all the nurses? I want some nurses!" The high point came as I dragged blankets and pillows from a laundry cupboard, shouting, "I'm sure there are some fucking nurses in here somewhere!"

That's why I plan to entitle my debut album "Anaesthetised By Gooseberries".

***

In later years, I visited Berlin many times, on account of having made friends with one Albrecht Schwab. By day, Schwab is a high-up and highly-paid (and respected, nay feared) tax official, by night, he is a natural party animal. Schwab could no doubt have a country mansion and a Mercedes, but chooses to live in a tiny fifth floor flat in the Moabit area and travel around on a battered bicycle. He is the world's most convivial and welcoming host (i.e. he likes a drink or two), so visiting him in Berlin is always an interesting prospect.

Almost every day, Schwab cycles to the Zoo park in order to play open air table tennis. But as he has grown older, he has also become more conservative. In 2001, the world governing body for table tennis decreed that the dimensions of table tennis balls were to be changed. Schwab was having none of this. He promptly bought up the capital's entire remaining stock of original table tennis balls, of which there were several thousand. Now Schwab has a couple of alternatives: He can play for the rest of his life without ever having to adjust his technique; or he can open a table tennis ball museum. But, knowing how canny he is, I suspect that he will flog the lot when their rarity value makes them much desired relics of a bygone age of ping-pong.

A couple of years before the Wall came down, Birgit and I spent a few days in Schwab's flat while he was away. Of course, the obligatory thrilling excursion to the Eastern sector of the city was irresistible, so we found ourselves on the Alexanderplatz, desperately searching, as usual, for something to spend our money on. This time, it was harder than ever, as the main department store seemed completely bereft of anything. The toy department had only one item, a yellow wooden duck with wheels, to be pulled along on a string. In the absence of any other possibilities, we purchased this item and took it for a walk around the Alexanderplatz.

The weather, unusually for Berlin, was sweltering, but even so, Birgit's choice of outfit was possibly not the most tactful. For reasons best known to herself, she wore a minuscule, Persil-white cotton dress which covered very little. The contrast with the drably-clothed East Berliners could hardly have been greater, and my memory of the Alexanderplatz was of being followed by hundreds of pairs of eyes displaying a mixture of scorn, fury, jealousy, disapproval, amazement, envy and lust, as we pulled our duck round the fountains. Uh-oh, I thought, we're gonna get arrested again.

When Schwab returned, he invited us out to one of his favourite haunts, which he had aptly christened "*Die Ruine*". This was a virtually derelict building, standing alone in the no-man's land near the *Lehrter Bahnhof*, just by the wall. Unaware of precisely what awaited us, I failed to warn Birgit against wearing "that" dress again.

Now one of my specialities in life is stumbling innocently into terrifying pubs which offer the promise of not emerging alive, but the *Ruine* beat them all. Every client had some kind of severe deformity or physical attribute which one tried not to look at for fear of causing offence: cross eyes, hare lips, unsuccessful tattoo removal attempts, missing digits, coke-destroyed nostrils, cauliflower ears, blackened remains of teeth, all were present. And everybody was drunk, not as in jolly slap-you-on-the-back drunk, but as in look-at-me-and-I'll-stab-you drunk.

We each ordered a bottle of beer (that being the only thing on the menu) and took in the surroundings. Doors hung off their hinges, every window was smashed, lumps of plaster fell off the walls and, the *coup de grace*, one wall was entirely missing, which meant that the passing motorists could look in. And, incidentally, what was it with those motorists? Why were they all driving so slowly? Ah, explained Schwab, that would be because that particular road was the *"Autostrich"*, where punters cruised for the plentiful prostitutes who, yes, now we came to look at it, were present in abundance. Well thanks, old pal, we're on the *Autostrich* and my wife is dressed in little more than a paper handkerchief.

As I looked around, I became aware of several things: The majority of the strangely deformed clientèle had Mohican haircuts, inordinate amounts of piercings of unlikely extremities of their bodies, and displayed a keen interest in Birgit's dress. The tall ones looked down it, the short ones looked up it and the rest tried to look through it. Me, I tried not to look at anything or anybody, for fear of, well, death.

The beer having been downed with unusual haste, we tiptoed out and attempted to hail a taxi, a risky and easily misinterpretable business in the circumstances.

I wonder if the *Ruine* is still there? They're probably selling bits of it in souvenir shops.

***

My last adventure in East Berlin took place immediately after the fall of the Wall. I'd gone to Berlin alone, in order to attend a music trade fair called BID ("Berlin Independence Days") in a doomed attempt to promote an album by a band called Automatic Dlamini. John Parish, the leader of that band, was also in town to perform in a showcase with an obscure instrumental outfit called the Guitar Orchestra. This event was to take place in an off the beaten track venue called the Franz Club, deep in what had, until recently, been the inaccessible Eastern Sector.

During the afternoon, I took the opportunity to walk through the Brandenburg Gate into the East unchallenged and unarrested, a novel experience. Wandering round Prenzlauer Berg, I found that nothing had changed at all. The Friday afternoon ritual was taking place, whereby large parts of the population claimed their wages and then immediately drank most of the money in the nearest bar. Schnapps and vodka were cheap and plentiful, and in a couple of places, you had to pick your way across senseless bodies spreadeagled on the floor.

For some reason, I felt the need to view the Wall from the Eastern side, a possibly futile but still grimly fascinating experience. You'd walk down a road and suddenly find that it came to an abrupt end. But, unlike on the Western side, you couldn't climb onto a platform and have a peek over the minefields and fences. All you could do was stare in bafflement at the breezeblocks forming a sudden and definite end to your freedom of movement. Still, the shops in Prenzlauer Berg did have a good stock of rare DDR-issue Billy Bragg albums. Dear Sir William had been the only UK rock artist whose records were sufficiently politically sound to be on sale in the East.

The Franz Club was terribly hard to find. A long and creaking S-Bahn journey was followed by a spooky walk through dark, deserted and threatening-feeling streets. Of course, all the record company people attending the BID had had the sense (and the money) to take taxis there. In a crazy piece of mis-matching, the Guitar Orchestra was supporting someone called David Cross, a violinist who had been in King Crimson for a while and was now promoting an awful prog-rock album on which he wailed and miaowed for hours on end. But he had fans, notably an American woman whom I misguidedly tried to interest in the Automatic Dlamini album. When she discovered that there were no famous names in the band (at least, not famous then, hee hee), she returned to extolling the alleged brilliance of David Cross.

No instrument is less suited to rock music than the electric violin. Even David Cross's fans started consulting their watches a few minutes into what was shaping up to be a marathon set, and, as it was getting on for 2 a.m., I decided to set off in search of a taxi. This was an optimistic thing to do. Vaguely thinking that there might be a taxi rank back at the S-Bahn station, I started to walk down the pitch-black, deserted cobbled road, keeping to the middle of it in order to avoid the shadows. I soon became aware that, behind me, there were some other echoey footsteps as well as my own. Someone was following me. Was it my long dreamed-of involvement in a Len Deighton novel or was it merely another person trying to escape from Death By Violin? I quickened my pace and so did my follower. I broke into a trot, and so did my follower. I began to run, and so did my follower. And then he called out:

"Hey, Sie!"

What? Surely the man from the Sex Bar in Eckernförde couldn't still be pursuing me after all these years? Still, at least he was using the polite form of address (a skinhead would certainly have said *"du"*), and the Stasi were no longer in action, as far as I was aware. Nevertheless, it was the equivalent of someone shouting, "Oi, you!" Would you have stopped? My heart was racing but at least I had the presence of mind to plan what I would do if he tried to mug me. An old-fashioned knee in the bollocks ought to do the trick.

"Mensch, halten Sie doch mal an. Ich tu Ihnen nichts!"

Surely a mugger would have expressed himself with more economy of words? This one was asking me to stop (well, that made sense) but also reassuring me that he wouldn't do me any harm. With knee primed for bollock-crunching, I stopped and turned round. In front of me stood an out of breath young man, quite respectable-looking. His body language was anything but threatening, and he immediately explained the situation. Did I want a lift anywhere? If so, he would be happy to drive me for a reasonable fee. It was my only option, he said, because there were no official taxis at that time of night and the S-Bahn wouldn't be open for several hours. How could I lose?

Well, were he to drive me to a lonely area, threaten me with a knife and steal my wallet, yes, I could lose. And since I had no wallet with me, he would no doubt stab me in a fit of fury and leave me bleeding in a gutter. But actually, he genuinely seemed like a nice chap and so, still on high alert, I accompanied him back to his car, where he politely explained that I should be aware that I wasn't insured. He also detailed the precise basis on which he would be charging me, and gave me a map with which to work out the most direct route.

On the way, he told me that he was in fact, a student, operating what was called a *"Schwarz-Taxi"* (an illegal, un-registered operation) in order to help to finance his studies. And he did, indeed, take me all the way back to Schwab's flat for a fraction of the normal fee, accompanied by some pleasant, informative, humorous conversation.

Which sort of goes to prove, once again, that you shouldn't automatically think the worst of people. Mind you, Schwab did tell me afterwards that I had been mad to accept the offer, and that he knew of plenty of such gullible passengers who had, in fact, been victims of the get-mugged-and-end-up-bleeding-in-the-gutter option. Ah well.

As for Berlin, it's still a great place to visit, especially if you like a crane-filled skyline and are into Techno music. But, along with the Wall, something of its mysterious charm has disappeared.

Chapter 6

A Nice Break

School trips, when you're in charge of them, are anything but a holiday. But that doesn't prevent your colleagues from asking, when you get back to school, "Did you have a nice holiday?" or, worse, "Did you have a pleasant break?". No, I have had neither a Nice Bloody Holiday nor a Pleasant Bloody Break.

During my time as a language teacher, I ran hundreds ... oh, all right, it just seemed like hundreds ... certainly scores of school trips to various unlikely parts of Europe. Every one of them was unpaid, in my holiday time. Every one of them had its fair share of frightening events and challenges, but few were as incident-laden as a Year Seven trip to the Grand Duchy of Luxembourg in 1979.

This was a trip which we "inherited", in that it had actually been arranged by a member of staff who had since departed, leaving us to take it over. Instead of hiring a coach, as any sane person would, this colleague had decided it would be educational to travel to Luxembourg by train. This with upwards of sixty ill-disciplined eleven and twelve year olds.

Every school trip has its token loopy pupil, but this one had two: Nora and Samantha. Their speciality was to hang around the teachers (because, obviously, none of the other children wanted anything to do with them) asking unbearable questions of the "Have we got there yet?" variety. But these two really surpassed themselves, favourite enquiries being "Why aren't they speaking English?" and "Is there a branch of Debenhams here?" And, as their temporary guardian, you had to bite back your natural instinct to reply, "Of course, there fucking isn't, you stupid cow" and instead assure her, "No, Samantha, the Luxembourg branch of Debenhams is temporarily closed for renovations".

When we arrived at Victoria Station and prepared to board the boat train, Samantha sat down on her rucksack, which action burst open the huge bottle of orange squash which her mother had thoughtfully packed. Blissfully unaware, Samantha crouched, head in hands, staring blankly into space as the contents trickled out and across the platform, looking for all the world as if she had wet herself. All the children naturally gathered round, pointing and sneering, while we teaching staff had to remove all Samantha's personal effects from her bag and wipe them down with the large supply of kitchen roll we had brought along for exactly such purposes.

There's something interesting about this, and in a way quite exciting for those who assume that children's lives are pre-destined on the basis of their background. When Samantha eventually left school, armed with virtually no qualifications, she almost immediately became pregnant. Naturally, we all tut-tutted and said things like "Whatever will become of that poor little mite?" We couldn't have been more wrong. Samantha's daughter was an absolutely charming girl, a talented academic high-flyer who ended up attaining a scholarship to Oxford University. Don't you think there's something reassuring about that?

Apart from an incident where we were tannoyed to remove two young miscreants from the lifeboats, we managed to keep the children reasonably under control on the boat and the train, despite the fact that we had a particularly unruly bunch of boys (the departed colleague had simply said 'yes' to everybody) and despite the other, sadly inevitable, fact that the seats we had reserved didn't actually exist, causing us to have to sit for several hours on the floor of the corridor of the train.

Nonetheless, we arrived at Luxembourg City intact and dragged our way through town, carrying our heavy luggage, in a bedraggled crocodile all the way to the Youth Hostel, which was situated at the bottom of a steep valley and populated by several large groups of Dutch schoolchildren.

It was at supper time that a terrible ritual, seemingly unique to UK schoolchildren, began. It was one we were powerless to stop. Far from being the kind of Youth Hostel where you had to fend for yourself, the Luxembourg hostel was run by a super-conscientious couple who prided themselves on the quality of their culinary expertise. Supper each day was a fabulous, almost gourmet affair, with at least three courses, using top quality fresh ingredients. But: There were no chips. There were no burgers. And, above all, there was no ketchup. This was intolerable for our pupils.

Contorting their faces into masks of horror, disgust and contempt, they would point at their plates and pronounce:

"Uuueeeaaarrrugh!"

in a high-pitched chorus.

"What's this?"

"I'm not eating that!"

"It's disgusting."

"Have you tried it yet, Kevin?"

"No."

"How do you know it's disgusting?"

"It just is."

Dear Samantha contributed one of her customary unanswerable questions:

"Mr Graaaa - ay?"

"Yes, Samantha?"

"Do I like this?"

"I don't know, Samantha. Why don't you try it?"

"Because I don't know whether I like it or not."

"But ... oh, never mind."

Outside in the corridor, there were machines selling sweets and Coca Cola. Invariably, the pupils would leave all their supper and immediately repair to these machines, into which they inserted all their pocket money.

Every morning, the kind wardens and their assistants would make up fabulous packed lunches consisting of filled rolls, fresh fruit and chocolate bars, for us to take on our daily excursions. For reasons which will forever remain unclear, these feasts were rejected as well:

"Look, Darren, there's a chocolate bar in there."

"Uuuueeeeargh!"

"But it's chocolate. You must like chocolate."

"No I don't. It's not English."

The chocolate was rejected because of its wrapper. At first, I used to get terribly angry at this, but you just had to come to terms with it or else spend your entire existence in a permanent condition of white rage.

On that first evening, after supper, we went for a brief walk around the city centre, pupils in tow. We stopped briefly at the Archduke's Palace, where the children indulged in the traditional sport of immobile sentry-baiting.

"Mr Graaaa - ay?"

"Yes, Samantha?"

"Does the Queen live here?"

"No, Samantha, the Archduke lives here."

"Is that the Archduke of Edinburgh?"

"No, it's the Archduke of Luxembourg."

"But if the Archduke of Edinburgh lives here ..."

"No, he ..."

"... why doesn't the Queen live here? Are they getting a divorce?"

"Well, ... oh, never mind."

Back in the Youth Hostel, it was bedtime. Maybe we should have known better than to put Samantha and Nora in the same room, but neither of them were naughty as such, so we put Samantha in the top bunk and Nora below. I went to bed early, on account of a rather frightening toothache which was beginning to make itself felt in that all-dominating way that toothache has of always arriving at the most inconvenient time.

In the early hours, a commotion occurred in one of the girls' dormitories. Nora had been snoring away on the lower bunk, lying on her back with her mouth open, revealing her huge adolescent tombstone teeth. Somehow, Samantha had managed to drop her heavy hairbrush from the top bunk, landing full square on Nora's vulnerable gnashers.

We staff arrived to find a scene reminiscent of the aftermath of a street brawl. It hardly seemed possible that an innocent hairbrush could inflict such carnage. One of Nora's teeth had been knocked out completely and the other dangled by a thread. Gushing streams of blood flowed down Nora's chin, across her chest and into an ever-deepening pool on the floor. The sheets of her bunk bed resembled a devil-worshipper's sacrificial altar.

We attempted to stem the flow by stuffing a towel into her mouth as she, not without cause, whimpered hysterically. Something would have to be done and Mike, the leader of the party, knew what it would have to be.

"Oliver, you've got toothache anyway. You'll have to stay behind tomorrow morning and take Nora to the hospital."

What? Oh yes, my toothache. I'd been temporarily distracted, but now I came to think of it, it was definitely getting worse. Despite the fact that the next day's outing was to the lovely nearby town of Echternach and its *"Gorges du Loup"*, I reluctantly declared myself willing to be the Good Samaritan.

Thus began a couple of days which, while I couldn't argue that they were absolutely typical of school trips, certainly weren't entirely untypical. It was just that rather more typical bits than usual were fitted into a slightly shorter period of time.

In order to picture the events, you have to have an idea of what we looked like. I was as near to normal-looking as I ever get, which means long-haired, unshaven and scruffily-dressed, undoubtedly a suspected paedophile. Nora was extremely pale, acne-covered and wore what turned out to be her only set of clothes, which after a few minutes developed what from a distance might have looked like a pop-art pattern but on closer inspection were actually splashes of blood. She clutched a sodden, bright-red handkerchief (which had at one time been white) to her mouth. I, in turn, was holding on to my cheek, which had become hugely swollen. I looked as if I had inserted

73

an entire unbitten orange into my mouth, rather like a suckling pig.

As we set off towards the bus stop, I took pity on Nora as she looked wistfully at a souvenir shop. Would she like me to buy her something to cheer her up? With as near to alacrity as circumstances permitted, Nora pointed at something which, even by the standards of useless, pointless souvenirs, was a triumph of inanity. When I now describe it, those readers who have seen one will say, "Oh yes, I know what he means", while those who haven't will say, "Nonsense, he's making it up".

It was a huge pencil, far too big to be used as a pencil is intended to be used. It was about the size of a small bicycle pump and was decorated with illustrations of the sights of the Grand Duchy of Luxembourg. At the end of the pencil was a little tin bell which didn't ring because it didn't have a clapper. But there was also something else. Attached to the end of the pencil was a little plastic pouch, about the size of your finger nail, and in the pouch were six tiny pencils, each about as big as a tin tack. So what you were purchasing was seven pencils, none of which could be used to write with.

This item was Nora's heart's desire, and so I bought it for her. As we traipsed on through the Luxembourg shoppers, Nora always several paces behind me, she carried her dingly-dangly pencil at all times. The clapperless bell made a vague rattling sound, so at least it helped me to know that she was still there. We didn't speak because **a:** Nora was monosyllabic anyway, and **b:** we were both so dentally challenged that speech would have been impractical.

The hospital, as hospitals tend to be, was on the outskirts of town, a journey involving two changes of bus (complete with incomprehensible rules for obtaining tickets, seemingly available nowhere). When we eventually arrived, we queued for a while before entering the time-honoured (as portrayed in Hal Ashby's 'Harold and Maude') "we can't prevent you from dying until we've seen your insurance form" ritual.

I waved the E111 form with reasonable confidence, because, with remarkable efficiency considering it was British, it had copious explanations for each country in a variety of languages. But to the Hattie Jacques-style frowning matron behind the desk, this was anathema. She sent us away to walk up and down the local dual carriageway for an hour while she researched the validity of the E111.

When we returned, Hattie announced with some triumph that we would have to go to the *"Caisse Malade"* to have the E111 validated. Ah, and where, pray, was the *Caisse Malade*? Of course, in central Luxembourg City, from whence we had just come. We climbed back on to the two buses (not at the same time, obviously) and arrived at the *Caisse Malade* just as the shutters were going up for an extended lunch hour.

At this stage, permit me to remind you of the scenario. The ashen faces, the pop-art clothing, the hankies and, of course, the dingly-dangly pencils.

It might have been appropriate to spend lunch hour eating lunch, but as neither Nora nor I were in any condition to masticate, this wasn't really an option. Conversation being impossible as well, I decided that we would walk through a nearby park, in the centre of which, the map said, lay the headquarters of Radio Luxembourg.

This was a pilgrimage I'd planned to make, in homage to my teenage heroes Kid Jensen, Stuart Henry et al. It wasn't much of a triumphant visit, because, of course, RTL had long since become Europe's repository for all things crap in the way of naff chat shows and soft porn. Plus, unsurprisingly, considering we looked like extras from Reservoir Dogs, they refused to let us past the outer entrance.

The Caisse Malade re-opened at 3 pm. After studying the form doubtfully for some minutes, the clerk placed an optimism-inducing stamp upon it and said we should take it back to the hospital. Two buses later (etc, etc), we were back with Hattie, who seemed taken aback that we had made such quick progress. Reluctantly adding her own stamp, she announced that the hospital had no facilities for dealing with our problems and that

I would have to ring a dentist.

"Couldn't you do that for me?" I pleaded.

You'd have thought that Sid James had made an indecent suggestion. This was not her job, replied Hattie. But she did go so far as to give me a list of dentists to ring. Could I use her phone? No, there's a call box in the foyer.

After several failed attempts, I was finally reduced to calling the terrifying-sounding *"Cabinet Dr Schneider / Dr Jungblut"*. Yes, we could make an appointment. Today? A weary sigh washed over my ear. Today? Out of the question. But they might fit us in if we turned up at eight o'clock the next morning.

Back in the hostel, dosed up with not very effective aspirin, I hoped for a quiet evening. Nora was not in a fit state even to say "Uuuuueargh" and so went to bed, bravely (or stupidly) re-billeting herself in the bottom bunk, which thankfully had undergone a change of linen. I lay down in my shared staff bedroom and sank into a deep slumber.

It must have been at about 2 am that I was woken by a more urgent than usual "Mr Graaa - ay!" My colleagues were already up and about, the corridor light was blazing and something in the way of a commotion was taking place. Peering from behind every dormitory door were several wide-eyed, open-mouthed young faces.

"There's been a prowler."

"Where?"

"In the dormitories."

"What's he done?"

"He's stolen Darren's money."

Darren, it turned out, had woken up to find someone beside his bed, removing some banknotes from his wallet. Now, Darren wanted justice."What are you going to do about it?" he demanded of the teaching staff.

"We'll have to make some enquiries," replied Mike, wearily. Within minutes, our staff bedroom had been turned into the

People's Court, as we took statements from a succession of likely candidates, all of whom had allegedly been seen by someone or other with their hands in Darren's wallet. As it became increasingly obvious that all of them were making their stories up, I allowed my attention to return to my increasingly agonising toothache.

We took it in turns to carry out sentry duty in the corridor. The pupils were hugely enjoying the opportunity for nocturnal activity and the rumours became ever more vivid:

"He had a knife, you know."

"He stole all the teachers' money."

"He had a black eye patch and a mask."

"He tried to rape Samantha."

"He threatened the teachers with a gun."

After all our interviews, it was hard not to conclude that probably nothing had happened at all, but we were wrong. In the morning, it emerged that the Dutch school party, too, had had a visitation in the night. It had been a young man who had broken into the hostel and had, indeed, systematically gone through the dormitories stealing from bags. One Dutch girl had woken up and caught him in the act. As a result, the hostel warden had apprehended him as he tried to make good his escape, scattering his booty as he ran.

As a consequence of all this and the resultant lack of even fitful sleep, Nora and I must have looked even more woebegone than usual as we set off at crack of dawn on our continuing search for the Holy Drill. As the rest of the group swapped rapist tales and prepared to set out, goodness knows why, on an excursion to the French industrial town of Metz, Nora and I joined the commuters of Luxembourg on the now increasingly familiar succession of buses, and arrived punctually at eight o'clock at the dungeon of Dr Jungblut.

"You may have to wait some time," warned the receptionist, making it clear that the good doctor was doing us an enormous favour and didn't really need to help us at all. As we waited, I helped Nora to do some German worksheets she had inexplicably brought along with her. As neither of us could speak, attempting to fill in the various prepositional phrases by the use of something akin to semaphore didn't really advance the cause of linguistic research.

Eventually, at ten o'clock, Nora was called in and I, a slave to my sense of duty, had to accompany her and hold her hand while Dr Jungblut embarked on the most extraordinarily convoluted and, to be fair, highly skilled operation. Both the completely detached and the nearly detached tooth were levered back into place and secured by something a bit like a barbed wire security fence. The wires which surrounded and supported the teeth were actually sewn through her gums. Naturally squeamish, I nonetheless watched the operation with a kind of appalled fascination and no little admiration.

To this day, I still occasionally bump into Nora in Winchester city centre, pushing a buggy and with all her teeth in fine fettle. She shows no more appreciation now than she did then, either of Dr Jungblut or me.

Finally, it was my turn. Dr Jungblut took a brief look at my swollen jaw, tut-tutted as if my suffering was all my own fault, wrenched my jaws apart, jabbed a cursory injection into my gum and, without waiting for it to take effect, produced a large pair of pliers and, in a searing few seconds of blind agony, pulled out the tooth. I didn't get any choice in the matter, but I didn't mind. That's how it is with toothache. You can pull the whole bloody lot out, for all I care, just as long as the pain goes away.

Meanwhile, over in Metz, the school group had arrived at the main station. As I had intended travelling to Metz later in the day to join them, Mike, the group leader, had the bright idea of leaving a message with the station announcer, to be broadcast at regular intervals. In that inimitable way that the French have of transposing Christian and surnames and refusing to attempt to pronounce them in a non-Gallic way, the tannoy was broadcasting to the world a repeated message:

"Gréh, Olivier ... Gréh, Olivier ... Gréh, Olivier est prié de se rendre immédiatement au Bureau de Renseignements."

The effort was, however, in vain, as I was at the time staggering out of Dr Jungblut's House of Horrors under strict instructions not to go anywhere near Metz, and still reeling from paying his gigantic bill from my scarcely solvent Eurocheque account.

It was vital to seek financial rescue back at the *Caisse Malade*, as well as to find a chemist in order to obtain the penicillin prescription the good doctor had made up. The customary lengthy safari by public transport brought the now glumly inevitable results: The *Caisse Malade* was shut, as were all the pharmacies and even all the banks. Yes, it was lunch time again.

There was nothing else for Nora and me to do but return to the Youth Hostel for the day. So we did. Except that there was one little matter I had forgotten, namely that youth hostels are always closed during the day. With a raging temperature, a hole the size of the Grand Canyon in my mouth, plus a companion who could have doubled as the Berlin Wall, I was no longer in any mood to be denied. I pounded on the door and yelled through the letter box until eventually the warden came and took pity on us. We both descended into a post-operative slumber.

The next day, we were well enough to accompany the rest of the group to the German city of Trier, where we all pretended to be lions and gladiators in the magnificent Roman amphitheatre. It was in Bernkastel, on the way to Trier, that another of those touching, almost life-affirming little scenarios happened. One of the young lads on the trip was called Shaun. He came from family circumstances that would have made it financially unthinkable for him to come on such a trip if the school fund hadn't been able to help out. We had made some sheets containing useful questions for the children to practise their German with, and sent them off into town for an hour. When Shaun returned, he was quite triumphant:

"Guess what," he told the teachers. "I asked twenty-three people the way to the Town Hall, and every single one of them knew where it was!"

It almost felt as if the trip was beginning at last, but the respite was brief. The following morning, we had to return to Dr

Jungblut for adjustments to Nora's metalwork. He was slightly critical of our failure to start our courses of penicillin.

"But it was impossible because ... oh, never mind."

The entire rest of the morning was spent queuing in the *Caisse Malade* until, after much scratching of heads and rifling through drawers in the same oddly haphazard way that detectives use when searching premises in films, they confessed that they had lost all trace of our documentation. Would we please return at 2 pm?

Running through the crowds (oh, by the way, remember the scenario: suckling pig, European Barbed Wire Mountain, dingly-dangly pencils, etc.), we arrived at the main square too late to meet the others, so had to settle for a second round of "Taunt The Sentries", except that neither of us was in any state to do anything other than gawp at them loopily. Accompanying Nora was giving me a taste of what an unhappy marriage must be like: Spending all your time with someone you have nothing in common with and not speaking.

During the afternoon, the money was finally retrieved from the *Caisse Malade*. Nora was feeling more normal and no longer in need of a permanent chaperone. Without any suggestion of a thank you, she returned to the bosom of Samantha and they both recommenced their "Uuuueeurghs" where they had left off. The kind warden made Nora a special clear soup which she could have drunk through a straw, but she merely said "yuk" and turned her back on it.

But at least we were able to rejoin the rest of the group for the final outing of the week, a visit to the Luxembourg Zoo. We had decided to do this at the last moment, encouraged by a colourful and glossy brochure which listed the many species of unusual animals to be found there, plus the establishment's commitment to conservation and the breeding of endangered species.

Because the map on the brochure was most definitely "not to scale", we had to walk for over an hour before we came to the zoo, which was obviously intended to have a Western theme. There was a tumble-down saloon, a couple of mangy ponies and a host by the name of Tony Bronco, complete with stetson, leather jerkin, six-guns and chaps. Tony Bronco turned out to be the sole member of staff. In fact, he was also virtually the only living creature there.

As the children traipsed round the various enclosures, the complaints began:

"Mr Graaaa - ay, all the cages are empty."

"I can't see any hippopotamuses in this pool, it's stagnant."

"Mr Graaaa - ay, it says here that there's supposed to be an elephant, but all there is is a pile of ..."

"Yes, yes, thank you, Darren."

But the kids were right. Apart from a couple of obviously malnourished antelopes, the only animals left were a few untrustworthy-looking wolves in the final enclosure. As we approached it, we met, trundling a wheelbarrow towards the wolves, the legendary gunslinger Tony Bronco. A brief glance at the wheelbarrow revealed it to be full of unidentified innards. Sticking out at various angles, rather like the sausages in Desperate Dan's Cow Pie, were limbs, hooves and bits of head of crudely chopped-up antelope.

Tony Bronco upended the wheelbarrow and the wolves fell upon its contents ravenously. It couldn't have been more obvious. He was feeding the last few remaining animals to the wolves, and we could only assume that, when the supply of antelopes ran out, the wolves would end up being fed to each other.

Mike entered forceful mode and demanded our money back. Tony Bronco was strangely reluctant to co-operate, until Mike mentioned that we were on excellent terms with the Luxembourg Tourist Office. Huffing and puffing, Tony refunded the entire day's takings (i.e. what we had given him in the first place).

As we trudged back towards the city, conversation was at its liveliest since the Night of the Rapist:

"Did you see that rhinoceros' tusk sticking out of the wheelbarrow?"

"I saw him shoot an antelope with his pistol and chop it up with his Bowie knife."

"He threatened to kill Mr Graaaa - ay and feed him to the wolves."

In the morning, we set out for the return journey. I, for one, felt relieved to be on the way home, but there was more dubious excitement to come. On the train, a young pupil called Wayne went to the toilet and, after a moment, we heard a blood-curdling scream emitting from the cubicle. Wayne was inside but the tips of two of his fingers were outside. Yes, he had shut his hand in the door.

It fell to Mike, as leader of the group, to hesitantly push open the door to reveal the kind of red-hued devastation we were now becoming almost blasé about. Sure enough, Wayne had virtually severed the tops of two fingers and sure wanted the world to know about it. What do you do in such circumstances? Of course, you pull the communication cord. My hand hovered within millimetres of it until someone pointed out, sensibly, that all that would achieve would be a stationary train in the middle of nowhere.

Now in a film, a man would push through the crowd at this point, calling, "Let me through, I'm a doctor." And guess what? Sometimes reality really does imitate art, because, within moments, that very man appeared and actually made that very announcement. And, surprisingly really, we didn't reply, "Piss off, this is no time for jokes."

The doctor (I didn't actually ask him what blood-curdling name he bore) patched Wayne up and said that it was essential that we should get him to hospital. The next stop would be Brussels, where we should arrange to have a taxi waiting for him, but before that, we would be passing through various smaller stations without stopping. The guard, who until then had hovered in the background looking nervous, suddenly had a light-bulb style idea, and disappeared into the toilet, emerging with a large roll of loo paper. His plan, in principle a sound one, was to wrap an SOS note in this object and hurl it out it the window at the next station.

A suitable missive was written (I can't remember in what language, Belgium is so confusing), inserted into the Blue Peter bit in the middle of the roll and sealed with sticking plaster from the first aid kit. As the next station approached, the guard took the roll in his hand, opened the window and threw.

Unfortunately, his aim was not true, so the roll bounced off the window frame and back into the train. But it wasn't long until the next station. As we approached it at speed, the guard's shot-putting technique was again shown to be lacking, as he threw too soon and we watched as the precious paper capsule came to rest on the tracks, several metres short of the station.

At this stage, announcing "I'm a golfer" (what this had to do with it was hard to see), Mike took charge of the situation. The third and final package was launched by him with an accuracy so deadly that it hit a gentleman on the platform, knocking his hat off. The only remaining worry was whether the man might merely think it had been the act of a vandal, thank his lucky stars it hadn't been a rock, and ignore it. To avoid this, we had written "*Ouvrez, s.v.p.*" in felt tip on the loo roll, hoping that French would be the appropriate language in that particular part of Belgium.

All was well. The ambulance awaited, and Mike descended with Wayne, officially handing over the mantle of Group Leader to me. Well, thanks a bunch. Penicillin-addled, still hardly capable of speech and distinctly queasy from the real-life experience of living through two Texas Chainsaw Massacres, I didn't cut the most authoritarian of figures. But duty was duty.

On the boat, the "lads" linked up with some drinking, off-duty squaddies who took exception when the staff tried to prise them from their attentions, threatening us with physical violence. As we disembarked, I didn't have even the slightest hope that I might be pleasantly surprised, and of course I was right. Not only were our reserved seats not reserved, but the whole boat train was full anyway, with the next one not due for two and a half hours.

Thus it was that we arrived back at school in the middle of the night. Even though we had alerted them by phone, many of the parents complained, clearly thinking that it was legitimate to blame the staff. Not a single person said thank you and of course, on the Monday, several colleagues asked, "Did you have a nice holiday?"

NO! PISS OFF!

But, back at Metz train station, to this very day, a ghostly voice can still be heard:

"Gréh, Olivier ... Gréh, Olivier ... est prié de se rendre au Bureau de Renseignements."

Chapter 7

Off the rails (1)

People who call themselves "writers" always sound a bit pretentious. After all, most people can write, can't they? It's a bit like calling yourself a "walker" because you're capable of walking down a street. Or calling yourself a ... no, let's not pursue that thought.

I'm certainly not a writer in that precious sense. All I do is compile text books for teaching languages. Nonetheless, as well as going abroad to take photos, you do actually physically have to write the stuff. So, while not being a "writer", I do have to spend my life writing. Does that make sense? No? Right, I haven't expressed myself properly, then.

Searching for what in the trade we call "realia" (i.e."real" items such as menus, tickets and brochures to use as illustrations and for Reading Texts) can be a dangerous business. This is how my unhealthy obsession with appropriating realia came about.

There are those who disparage the use of realia as "Bus Ticket Teaching", but any traveller will attest to the frequent necessity of understanding some information presented in the written form. In a tourist office, for example, you can go in with your carefully-prepared question but you most likely won't understand the quickly-spoken answer. Much better to retire to your hotel room with a leaflet and a dictionary and work things out in your own time.

Language teachers know this, and few can resist the allure of collecting realia. Observe them as they stagger off the cross-channel ferries, rucksacks stuffed with rain forests' worth of Intermarché leaflets and brochures about the *"distractions"* of Bordeaux. All of these pathetic creatures are, like me, hopeless bus ticket junkies.

You can get hooked horrifyingly quickly. Within hours of discovering a particularly alluring listings magazine on a midwinter ferry to the North Sea island of Wangerooge, I was a gibbering addict. Not that there were many bus tickets on Wangerooge (there are no roads) but regretfully my family was to see little of me in the subsequent days, which were spent in a frenzy of charging in and out of information bureaux, swimming pools, places of entertainment, eating establishments and such. Not, you understand, in any way connected to actually using any of these places for their various intended purposes, but merely in order to emerge triumphantly clutching fistfuls of leaflets. A lifetime's adventure had begun.

A bus ticket junkie suffers much the same torments as any other addict, among them a constant fear of being discovered and exposed. One of the first things I learnt was that any scorn for collectors of realia was completely misplaced. Finding the right stuff is actually extremely difficult. You need thirty Problem Pages to find one usable letter. You need two supermarket carrier bags full of brochures to find one suitable advert. So, when you find that the restaurant you are in has the perfect menu you have been seeking for the past three months, furtive behaviour is unavoidable. First, you slip it under your place mat. Then, choosing your moment carefully, you try to appear as if casually sliding menus into rucksacks were the most natural thing in the world. Paranoia rules. It's no good asking for permission. What if they say no? Then you'll have lost all chance of obtaining this prize specimen because they'll be watching you like hawks until you leave.

How is it possible to get in such a state? Of course they'd let you have a copy of their menu, and with the greatest of pleasure. Ha! Don't be so sure! Since my experience at Magnet, a supermarket in the North German backwater of Elmshorn, I can believe anything. I had naively thought that it was a citizen's right to take photos of more or less anything public, but the security guard who marched me off, literally by the scruff of my neck, to the manager's office clearly thought differently. Even then, I wasn't worried. It wasn't as if I was the paparazzi. Surely, after explaining my innocent reasons for taking photos of signs saying things like "Fruit and Vegetables", I would be allowed to continue.

This was not the case. The grilling I received revealed that they were convinced that I was a spy representing a rival chain of supermarkets. I was ignominiously shown the door without further ado. The only remaining pleasure lay in announcing that I no longer intended to purchase the trolleyful of goods I had accumulated.

That this humiliating defeat was no flash in the pan was confirmed when I took a more legitimate approach with the Wertkauf hypermarket in Bremen. Having written in advance, I made an appointment to see the manager and explained my mission to him. Sorry, he said, but nobody was allowed to photograph his store. Why not? There then followed the classic exchange of encounters with German authority:

"Es geht nicht." ("It's not allowed.")

"Warum geht es nicht?" ("Why isn't it allowed?")

"Weil es nicht geht." ("Because it isn't allowed.")

Luckily, no such problems were found at the Continent store in Cherbourg, unless you count a small boy who, having fewer inhibitions than the scores of mystified adults following my seemingly crazy activities, demanded, *"Pourquoi vous faites ça?"* He seemed quite satisfied with the response, *"Ah, je suis anglais"*. His elders, meanwhile, contented themselves with speculating about what kind of kick I could be getting from photographing a sign saying, in French, *naturellement*, "Ladies' Underwear". Never can Asterix's observation *"Ils sont fous, les anglais"* have seemed more apt.

Once you have collected the various leaflets, you have to write to the numerous copyright holders for permission to reproduce their materials. Far from the surly attitudes of supermarket managers, people from Tourist Offices have greeted my requests with nothing but the utmost support and enthusiastic interest. The lady from the *Meerwasser-Freizeitbad* swimming pool on Wangerooge, for example, was thrilled at the notion of hundreds of British schoolchildren studiously working out what time on a Wednesday the mixed sauna closed. Whether she would have been so keen if she had known the reactions of the studious

British schoolchildren to her island's name is not so certain. One spotty teenager was overheard to ask,

"What the fuck does 'Wanker-Oogie' mean? Is it some kind of sexy dance?"

Obscure villages in the Pyrenees have written expressing great joy at the free publicity, while bigger towns, with similar thoughts in mind, have showered me with unrequested and unwanted further information (enough, incidentally, at the last count, to fill three sheds and one attic). Only one incident made me feel awful. The publicity manager of a steam railway line in Luxembourg sent eight closely-written longhand pages detailing the history of his enterprise, apparently believing me to be closely interested in the intimate details of his locomotives. To salve my conscience, I went out and bought him a book about steam lines in Britain.

Most difficult of all is getting hold of recorded material for use on Listening Comprehension tapes. A mission to Normandy to collect background ambient noise confirmed this. Standing on the corner of a Rouen street in the rain was okay, even if the microphone sticking out from under my coat must have looked like a Luger, such were the horrified glances I received. And I nearly got myself squashed to a pulp trying to record the sound of a streetcar pulling up at a tram stop in Bremen. Something even more unexpected, however, was the discovery in Le Havre of a silent supermarket. Yes, in *Auchan* there is no muzack, the tills neither bleep nor buzz, and even the trolleys are well-oiled. It's actually all very pleasant, unless you're a bus ticket junkie.

Avid listeners to The Archers on Radio 4 (and, of course, to the cassettes accompanying French teaching courses) will be aware that the sound of a restaurant is an incessant clinking of knives on plates and tinkling of glasses. Wrong! As we discovered when trying to get restaurant noises in Honfleur. For a start, it was hard to decide where to put the microphone. On our table was not a good idea, since the sound of four people talking English was hardly going to conjure up an image of a bijou-Bistroette; so in the end, it ended up in my sister's handbag, on the floor, pointing towards the next door table. So far, so good. Next, it was necessary for us to remain silent for ten minutes, which is fine until you have to do it. Four people sitting round a table in a restaurant and not saying a word for ten minutes must have looked and sounded pretty strange. It was also damned difficult not to giggle, especially as (having discovered that restaurants are not, in fact, filled with tinkling and clanking noises, because the diners are trying to avoid doing just that), we were forced to set up a suitable cacophony by scraping knives on empty plates and hitting empty glasses with forks.

It was on one of our famous Luxembourg trips that Mike and I had an interesting encounter with an employee in the city's tourist office. Because he took such a liking to us, he insisted on pressing upon us every leaflet in his not inconsiderable stockroom, in triplicate. Mike's rucksack was so heavy that he exited the office leaning backwards at an angle of 45 degrees.

But last year, needing a particular type of text, I suddenly remembered this incident. Sure enough, in a dusty corner of the attic, almost obscured by the remains of a wasp nest, was a bag of leaflets, three of each, in mint condition. A real bus ticket junkie, you see, never throws anything away. You never know when it might come in useful.

So you have your realia, now you have to collate the materials and physically write the exercises and all the other things that need to be done to transform a leaflet advertising, for example, the Berlin Museum of Table Tennis Balls into something useful to a language learner.

Theoretically, you could do this at home, but home has certain disadvantages. Number One is the phone. You can switch on the answering machine, but mightn't the call be urgent? In fact, it's your delightful but garrulous mother, so that goes on for an hour. Or it's some bastard trying to convince you that you should buy your gas from an electricity company or your electricity from a gas company. You get so mad that it takes you an hour to calm down.

Distraction Number Two is BBC Radio Five Live. How they

manage to make their station unfailingly fascinating for 24 hours a day is a mystery, but somehow they do it. So you pretend that the radio is broken and, before you know it, just checking the TV news headlines at five to nine, you're into bloody *Kilroy*, then, Lord help you, *Trisha*, and then (no one can help you now) a succession of identical German chat shows on RTL presented by people with names like Uschi, Berndt and Karin. And while you know that mindless discussion on topics like "My Dog Is A Lesbian", "My Mother's Sleeping With The Man Doing The Garden Makeover" and "My Breasts / Buttocks Are Too Big / Small / Saggy", it only takes a second to get hooked. And then it's lunchtime.

So that's how I came across the Euro Domino, a method of travelling which, like the game of dominoes itself, seems simple but is not always as straightforward as it appears. The theory was that trains are quiet places where you can work undisturbed. The scenery is normally undistracting (here I made major errors by going for the Alps and the Sierra Nevada, getting practically nothing done at all). And you can cover enormous distances without anything distracting your attention from the work in hand.

Apart, of course, from one little thing: those pesky little items that play tunes in people's pockets:

"Je suis dans le train."

"Ich bin im Zug."

"Estoy en el tren."

Ah yes, in the vital matter of overhearing other people's mobile phone conversations, I am truly multilingual. Eventually, instead of getting apoplectic, I took to taking along a personal stereo and getting my revenge by annoying everyone with those incessant little distant percussive swishing effects.

A Euro Domino is a train ticket which will take you anywhere you want to go. You can buy them for individual countries and for any number of days within a month. This theoretically means that you can explore a country in its entirety for a set fee, travelling to a different city or region each day. In the main, it doesn't really help you to get far off the beaten track, since there are lots of places that don't have train stations. Still, you can always look out of the window.

I'd read an article about Swiss trains, their reliability, their punctuality, their frequency and their ability to scale mountains. It sounded perfect, but the cheap flight only went to Frankfurt, so I opted for a ticket covering both Germany and Switzerland.

The first leg took me from Frankfurt to Lucerne. No idea why, it just jumped out of the map as a place which might be quite nice. The Tourist Office at the station was quiet, but obviously something was going on, as employees were bustling hither and thither, laying out trays of nibbles.

"What's happening?" I enquired of the impeccably well-groomed young man at the desk.

"This is a new office which is opening today and we're having a reception this afternoon for the mayor and the press. Would you like to come, as you're our first ever customer?"

This was truly an unrefusable offer. I spent the afternoon imbibing champagne and being interviewed by TV and radio crews about what I thought of Lucerne and the Tourist Office's services. I knew nothing about either but nevertheless waxed lyrical about the magnificence of both.

Marc (this was the clerk's name) digested my request for somewhere quiet but beautiful and recommended Engelberg, to which there was a train in the evening. It immediately became clear just how accurate the article about the brilliance of Switzerland's trains had been. It left at the very second it was meant to (you could watch the station clock ticking down) and it travelled through the most chocolate boxy villages imaginable as it climbed higher and higher into the mountains.

Some people say Switzerland is almost too perfect. I say what's the point of making a judgement that something is perfect and then moaning about it? The smart little snow-covered chalets with their balconies, the impeccable cleanliness and tidiness of everything, the pervasive air of prosperity and contentment ... yes, I'll have some of that, *danke schön*.

After about an hour, the train stopped and there were a few clanking noises. Out of the window, I could see that the method of traction was being altered. We were changing from just being pulled along a track to being hauled up a sheer mountain side by a chain. In the same train! The other couple of passengers were obviously regulars and didn't even glance up from their books. I wanted to nudge them violently and say, "Christ, look what's happening, isn't it wonderful?" but decided against it.

Up and up we went, ears popping, almost vertically through the pine forests.The train arrived in Engelberg (Angel Mountain, very apt) in the dark. There was absolutely no one about, no one to ask where the hotel might be, yet everything around me was picture postcard ideal: the half-timbered houses, the glittering shop windows, the sense that the shadows behind them contained massive Alpine peaks.

Suitcases with little wheels don't take to every surface, and sheet ice is one of the less favourable ones. Being stupidly unprepared, I wasn't wearing remotely suitable shoes, so when I eventually found a wooden sign with the name of the hotel and an arrow, it was disturbing to see that it pointed up quite a steep hill. But I made it, and the interior of the "Hotel Alpenclub" was exactly what you'd imagine it would be like: big wooden tables, a crackling log fire and gigantic mugs of beer. I was the only guest. My room was across a snowy courtyard and contained a TV which seemed to show nothing but mildly pornographic movies. I didn't mind that at all.

Marc had recommended for the next day an excursion to the Rigi. Pardon? Apparently it was a mountain, Rigi by name but Bigi by nature. The journey entailed going back down the Engelberg mountain to Lucerne, across the lake and up the Rigi by funicular. Everywhere I went, there was no one else about. This was a mystery to me. It was January, surely the height of the ski season? But it was term time all over Europe and thus there were no tourists.

The journey across the lake was surreal. I was the sole passenger aboard a large steamer, most of which was taken up by an opulent dining room. I felt sorry for the white-coated waiter and ordered, in succession, a tea, a coffee and a hot chocolate. It was like having your own personal butler.

The Swiss understand what an integrated transport system is. Not only had the boat been timed to leave Lucerne to coincide with the arrival of the train from Engelberg, but it was also timed to arrive just in time for the departure of the funicular, which waited at the end of the landing stage. I had to walk, oh, all of twenty metres.

The little two-carriage funicular train actually had some other occupants, in the form of young primary schoolchildren going home for lunch. The train stopped at individual houses to drop them off. As the children were all engrossed in their homework, I thought I'd join them by doing some "writing", but was distracted by the scenery, which was so beautiful I felt quite tearful.

Suddenly, everything went grey. Bugger, I thought, there's going to be a storm and everything will be ruined. But seconds later, we emerged into shatteringly bright sunshine and I realised that we had burst through the clouds. The peak of the Rigi reared up above us, the train stopped and a path led temptingly towards the summit.

The expression "Top of the World" is a bit of a cliché, but how else could you describe it? Looking down, the clouds dared you just to take off and float down into them. That, however, would have been silly, so I opted to follow an idea suggested on a map board and walk down to the next station. I could have hired a toboggan but, not knowing what lay around the next corner, was scared.

My ridiculously unsuitable footwear meant that I fell flat on my back three times, winding myself on each occasion. This is where a rucksack can be a life-saver, provided you don't put anything precious into it, or anything breakable such as a glass bottle, ooh, that's a painful thought.

The Rigi. Those aren't islands, they're mountain tops.

More adventurous than me, a group of young snowboarders were taking it in turns to hurtle down the mountainside, catch the train back up and do it again. As they sat on the platform, they rolled a gigantic joint and passed it round, presumably to heighten the experience. That looks fun, I thought. I also thought that such uninhibitedly public drug taking was not at all what I would have expected to see in Switzerland. Isn't it only a few years since women were given the vote?

The next day, I decided to move on from Engelberg. One problem with a Euro Domino is that, if you find a particular place so wonderful that you wish to stay there, you are wasting the mobility that you have paid for. So I looked at the map and recognised the name Grindelwald, much mispronounced by David Vine, as in:

"And here in Grin-dell-warld, it's the turn of Britain's Martin Bell, and ... oh, he's fallen over."

Getting to Grindelwald entailed changing at Interlaken (*In-turr-lawkin*, yes, thank you, David), and I decided to check out the town. This was a bad move, because the station was about a mile from the town centre, which turned out to be a very flat and boring place consisting of closed casinos and cafés full of frowning pensioners. Just for the record, thesurface, for the dragging of wheeled suitcases, was gravelly and uncooperative.

I knew I was going to hate Grindelwald as soon as the train arrived. Hoardings advertised cigarette companies and other sponsors of some ski event or other. Bronzed Adonises clumped about with big boots and and skis over their shoulders. And the Tourist Office was ages from the station (this time back to the sheet ice). I was offered a room in a guest house which looked nice in the picture, so I said that I'd have it.

What I hadn't realised was that it was several hundred metres up the side of the mountain. My footwear was not up to the challenge, so I slithered about, mainly on my knees, pushing the suitcase in front of me. Periodically, the case and I would slide back to where we had started, helplessly grabbing at a splinter-filled handrail. It was horrible, and so was the guest house. There was an ugly, growling Rottweiler and a glowering landlady who looked at me with contempt and claimed not to be expecting me (although I'd listened to the call being made at the Tourist Office). Uppermost in my mind was the fact that there was no bar there. Half the fun of Euro Dominoing is going out for something to eat and drink in the evening. However would I get back up that hill after a few beers? I resolved not to give the landlady the pleasure of being horrible to me any longer, sat astride my suitcase and tobogganed back into town on it. In-turr-lawkin it would have to be, then.

Interlaken has two bits, one on either side of the river. At the station, there was a large board with a phone, from which you could call a hotel. A man at the other end assured me that his hotel was only five minutes from the station. See you in five minutes, then, I said, and then spent half an hour pacing up and down roads which bore no resemblance to the directions he had given me. I called again.

"Sorry, I can't find you."

"Where are you?"

"At the station."

"Which station?"

"Which station? Interlaken, of course."

"Oh ..."

It only bloody turned out that Interlaken had two bloody stations. And that, with hideous inevitability, I was at the wrong one.

A long and expensive taxi ride later, I arrived at the hotel, gratified to find that, despite being in a grotty area, it was pleasingly Swiss-perfect. Again, I was the sole guest, and when I entered the bar for a beer, the owner and a white- coated, white-hatted chef were waiting expectantly in the kitchen doorway. I had actually planned to go out somewhere for supper, but proved incapable of being so cruel to them. This seemed an ideal opportunity to sample the much-recommended Swiss cheese fondue, advertised on the wall as the speciality of the house.

Well, all I can say is that Swiss cheese fondue is over-rated. You get a vat of melted cheese, a stick and a plateful of stale bread. And that's it. You dip the bread into the cheese, slurp it and watch strings of it attach themselves to your shirt. On the gourmet excitement meter, it registers nought out of ten. And it gives you nightmares.

In the morning, I travelled through unbelievably beautiful lake and mountain scenery to Geneva. I found this place a bit spooky. There had just been some kind of demo, and large numbers of police patrolled the cobbled streets. The bars in the old town were full of very loud-mouthed and very well-heeled teenage offspring of American diplomats. It all felt a bit unreal, and I finally decided I didn't want to be in Geneva when I stepped in some dog shit. Never stay in a town which offends your nostrils.

It was time to head back to Frankfurt. Looking at the map, I suddenly had an idea. Almost directly en route lay Rothenburg ob der Tauber, the fairytale walled town I had visited all those years earlier on the *Fahrt*. Could it possibly be as beautiful as I remembered? There was only one way to find out.

The journey involved several changes at a series of deserted and dingy junctions. German trains are efficient, yes, but they can also be austere, with uncomfortable, straight-backed, plastic-covered seats to which your skin sticks. Rothenburg was at the end of a branch line and the station was dark and freezing, occupied only by a couple of daunting skinheads, who looked at me in an unfriendly way. Luckily, a taxi cruised by and took me to a smart little hotel. But that evening, something happened of which I am not proud. Well, all right, amid the shame, I am just a little bit proud.

Outside a quaint-looking restaurant, I spotted something extremely rare in Germany, a vegetarian menu. This was very tempting, so in I went. I was, guess what, the only customer. I ordered the vegetarian menu and waited for the starter, a mixed salad, to arrive. I was "writing", so had already dug my fork into the salad before I realised that it contained, in fact, a large number of lumps of smoked ham. Unnerved, I called over the waitress.

"It says this is a vegetarian menu."

"Yes."

"But there's ham in it."

"Yes, but there are several vegetables. Look, there are tomatoes, onions, lettuce ..."

"But a vegetarian menu shouldn't have meat in it."

"You can pick out the meat and just eat the vegetables."

"But ... oh, never mind."

So I just left it. But the fact that she neither apologised nor offered me any alternative awakened the devil in me. Oh, and the fact that she stood there filing her fingernails and looking at her watch, and had stupid false eyelashes. There, that's justification enough, isn't it?

I sat at the table, "writing" and ordering beer after beer as it got later and later and the waitress stood around, sighing pointedly and tapping her no doubt smelly feet. Eventually, she announced that she was going home and placed the bill on the table, saying that I should pay the night porter (as the restaurant was also a hotel).

I fully intended to pay the bill, honest I did. It was just that, when I got to the exit, the aged night porter was fast asleep, snoring loudly. No one will ever know, I reasoned, and tip-toed out of the door. A few paces down the street, I heard the enraged voice of the night porter:

"Hey, Sie!"

Oh, for crying out loud, not again.

"Come back, you haven't paid!"

I knew I could run faster than him, so I plunged down a side alley, with the porter's shouts of "Stop thief" (literally) ringing in my ears. I crouched behind a dustbin until all was quiet. Considering the surroundings, it all felt very much as if I was actually involved in some gruesome Grimm's fairy tale.

In the morning, I became aware of the full enormity of what I had done. Off-season Rothenburg ob der Tauber probably didn't have a surfeit of crime and I imagined fleets of green-suited *Polizei* cruising the streets in Mercedes patrol cars, searching for me. I made sure I wore totally different clothes and stuffed my pony tail up inside my cap. But the wheeled suitcase probably gave me away. Big fat cobbles, by the way, wheelie rating: 0 /10.

At the station, the skinheads had disappeared. Being probably the only potential criminals in Rothenburg ob der Tauber, they had no doubt been arrested for my crime. Sorry, guys.

Chapter 8

Off the Rails (2)

In general, my game of Dominoes had gone so well that I was eager to make it an annual event. The following January, therefore, I bought a Euro Domino for France, the excuse being that my daughter Annabel was studying for A-level French and we had arranged for her to spend a week with a family in Paris. She was perfectly capable of going on her own, but I pronounced that she required a chaperone for the journey. The Eurostar was fully booked, but they offered to upgrade us to First Class for very little money and three coupons from the *Independent on Sunday*, so who could have resisted?

You could hardly imagine a greater contrast than that between South West Trains and the Eurostar. At Waterloo, you climb out of the filthy, litter-ridden, urine-smelling slam door catastrophe of a train from Winchester, walk a few metres and suddenly you're in the lap of luxury, welcomed by uniformed hostesses and plied with champagne (it surely can't be real champagne, can it?). Over your little table lamp, you could almost, if you didn't look out of the window, be on the Orient Express. Annabel, who has a taste for luxury, was in paradise as a succession of poncily-named dishes was placed before us.

It's fashionable to knock UK railways (in fact, I've just done it) and compare them unfavourably with everyone else's. Well, I'm here to say that French railways are pretty crap as well. That evening, I joined my Parisian host on the internet to make some plans. I wanted to visit a friend in Troyes, a couple of hours south east of Paris, and then continue on towards Avignon, more or less in a straight line. Even in England, such a trajectory wouldn't have been unreasonable.

"You won't be able to do it," said my host.

"What do you mean?"

"You'll have to come back via Paris."

"But that's the exact opposite way to where I want to go."

"I know, but I bet that's what you'll have to do."

He then went into a convoluted historical explanation of why the French rail system is totally Paris-centric, laying the blame, for reasons I didn't quite follow, firmly at the feet of Napoleon Bonaparte.

The SNCF website proved my host right and me wrong. To get from Troyes to Avignon, I would indeed have to return to Paris, cross from the *Gare de l'Est* to the *Gare de Lyon* by metro, and start again. All of which I did, but as I arrived at the *Gare de Lyon*, it was clear that all was not well. It was crammed full of gesticulating passengers and a healthy contingent of riot police. A few enquiries elicited the information that the lines were being blocked by nurses, striking for improved pay and conditions.

And it was true, because, by standing on tiptoe, I could, in fact, make out a substantial number of not-unattractive uniformed nurses sitting on the tracks, waving banners and preventing any trains from entering or leaving the station. It was rather sweet, but also a little inconvenient, in view of the fact that my friends were waiting for me in Avignon.

These were no ordinary friends. They were Eddie Hardin, a successful seventies rock musician and cohort of, among others, the Spencer Davis Group and Deep Purple, and his lovely wife Liz. In the immortal words of Bill Wyman, Eddie could truthfully sing, *"Si, si, je suis un rock star, je avez un résidence, et je habitez là, dans le South of France"*. Being slightly in awe of Eddie (as well as hoping to be appointed as his biographer), this was not a person I wished to upset.

As it happened, it didn't really matter. Engrossed in their shopping, they hardly seemed to notice that I was two hours late, but I did come across an interesting scam at Avignon station. A worried-looking young girl came up and asked me if she could borrow my phone card. She explained that she wanted to contact her parents, about whom she was concerned because thay had failed to pick her up. Poor thing, I thought, proferring my still nearly full card. I turned round for a second and she was gone. Clever stuff, eh? Or I'm just a dork.

The couple of days I spent with Eddie and Liz didn't enable me to do much "writing", but they sure were fun. That part of Provence is apparently stuffed with British expats, and a newly-arrived couple were invited over to supper. I was wide-eyed and starstruck as the wife turned out to be George Michael's interior designer, while her husband, Harry the Hairdresser, claimed to have been Jimi Hendrix's hair stylist. He said he had done Jimi's hair on the evening he died. Christ! I was in the presence of royalty!

I planned to make my way to Montpellier and catch the TGV back to Paris, but some instinct, I don't know what, made me decide to check, in the Provençal village of Uzès, on the train times from Montpellier. The lady in the SNCF office (pretty cool that there was one, considering that Uzès doesn't even have a train station) looked doubtful. Even though the proposed journey was three days hence, she was sure there would be no seats.

"But look, here's my Euro Domino. I've paid for it. Surely it entitles me to travel."

"Not without a TGV reservation."

"But how else can I get back to Paris?"

"Hmm ... you could always catch a plane from Nice."

"Whaaat? But my Eurostar reservation ... my daughter ... oh God, what shall I do?" I blubbed.

"Un instant, s'il vous plaît."

Her computer was flashing something at her. Someone had just cancelled a reservation on the 6 a.m. TGV from Montpellier. Did I want it?

"Oh yes, yes. Let me buy you a drink. Let me buy you some flowers!"

As she wearily tapped the information into her computer, the clerk's eyes conveyed a clear message: typical expat. Can't hold his Pernod.

Anyway, about those so-called wonderful French trains. The one from Nice to Montpellier was almost unbearably spartan and slow, breaking down twice as it took nearly an entire day to cover a distance which was, according to the map, almost walkable. Well, you know what I mean. And as for the TGV, well, when it's full, it's as cramped as the tiniest aeroplane. Plus, in this case, either side of me were two pompous male actors, on their way to Paris to perform in a play. They rehearsed their lines across me at deafening volume and seemed not in the least concerned by the pointed percussive swishing of my headphones.

Back on the Eurostar, the return journey was far less pleasurable. Opposite us sat an upper-crust middle-aged English couple. He wore a checked sports jacket, cavalry twills and Hush Puppies, while she was ugly as shit. Goodness knows why they were still together, far less going on holiday with each other, because they obviously hated each other's guts. The bitter-shrew-faced woman complained about every possible aspect of the journey: the speed, the comfort, the food, the drink and, of course, us (she disapproved of the fact that Annabel didn't want to sit up straight). It was so tense that I got close to exploding:

"Shut up, you revolting old cow. If your henpecked husband hasn't got the guts to say it, I will!"

But of course I didn't say it. I held my tongue until we could re-mount the recently-vandalised South West Train and return home.

***

Gluttons for punishment, some people. By the following June, I had regrouped sufficiently to embark upon a Euro Domino assault upon Spain, nominally in order to take photos for a new Spanish teaching book.

The bucket shop telephonist couldn't believe her ears.

"Anywhere in Spain?"

"Anywhere."

"Goodness."

Great! She could see I was an international jet setter. Within minutes, I had booked a flight to Barcelona. Within further minutes, I had unbooked it again, following advice from my kindly Mexican neighbour that the language in Barcelona is actually Catalan. Whoops! And so it was that I found myself booked on Swordfish Airways. I have changed the name in order to protect the guilty, but just let's say that if Easy Jet's motto is "No Frills", then the motto of Swordfish is (or was, since they have unsurprisingly gone out of business) "Frills? What are they then?". Or, to paraphrase Steely Dan, "Can't Buy A Frill".The destination was Madrid.

"It'll end in tears," pronounced my wise wife, "but at least it'll be an adventure."

The adventure began at 8.10 am on a deserted Shawford Station, one stop down the line from Winchester, from whence the tortuous journey to Gatwick was to commence. When the train hadn't arrived fifteen minutes after it was due, I calculated that I would no longer be able to make the connection at Cosham and would thus miss my flight. Relaxation exercises were commenced, after which I ran to a phone box and phoned home.

"Can you take me into Winchester?"

On the way, I used our newly-acquired mobile to ring the enquiry office. Yes, I could still make it via Clapham Junction. So let's get this straight: I have never really minded mobile phones at all.

The man in the ticket office was abrupt. "Bastards," he spat. I was about to be offended, but he continued: "The people who run this bloody train company don't care about their passengers at all. They just shrug their shoulders and deny responsibility. Here, fill in this complaint form. Don't forget!"

It turned out that the train had been cancelled, but since Shawford station is unmanned - er, unpersonned -, there was no way of letting passengers know. It's the rail company's way of functioning: Make it as inconvenient as possible to use the small stations, then close them, citing lack of demand.

I stood all the way to Clapham Junction, successfully negotiated the puddles of urine in this most desolate of stations and ended up on the 9.03 to Bognor Regis, in which I sat on a piece of recently-expectorated chewing gum and got a stiff neck from a perishing draught from the rickety door.

Gatwick, with its bustling crowds of happy youngsters heading off on package holidays, seemed almost welcoming. Unfortunately, Swordfish Airlines had a bit of a whammy waiting: There would be a delay, a long delay. How long, no one knew; please watch the screens. This was difficult, as the flight was nowhere mentioned on any screens.

In McDonalds, I noticed an attractive young family I'd met in the queue. They were stuffing themselves with McNuggets. "Swordfish Airlines are offering refreshment vouchers," they explained.

Off I trotted to collect mine. A small gaggle of worried passengers was gathered round listening to the latest information. Sweaty-browed and peppering his sentences with expressions like "at the end of the day" and "at this moment in time", the official explained the problem. The plane was currently in Lyon and had lost a wheel (bloody hell!). A wheel would be flown out to France, fitted, and the plane would then fly to Gatwick to collect us. We could expect an update at 3.30, earliest possible take-off time being 5 pm. It was 10.30 in the morning. To think I'd been worried about checking in late!

A couple with a small child were worried about the late arrival time. Could the airline phone through to Madrid for them?

"I'm sorry, madam, but we don't have an outside line."

Pardon? A high-tech airline doesn't have an outside line? And another thing (not strictly relevant, but I can't find anywhere else to fit it in): Have you ever noticed how the tannoy systems on aeroplanes never work properly? If they can't even get a P.A. to work, what about the engines? Oh God, recommence relaxation exercises!

A cup of coffee would be nice. I approached a huge coffee emporium and asked for a decaff. The waiter stared at me insolently:

"Haven't got any."

I had thought this was a coffee shop, but remained polite.

"Where can I get a decaff?"

"Nowhere."

Instead, I paid £1.85 for a caffeine-filled cappuccino which effectively negated the effects of the relaxation exercises.

What on earth was there to do for six and a half hours at Gatwick? It's full of useful things such as knicker shops (I've got loads of knickers), tie shops (I don't wear ties) and sunglasses shops (I already had sunglasses). There was nothing for it but to have a kip.

I had a jacket full of money and a bag full of important things like cameras. I wanted to sleep but I was frightened they'd get stolen. In the end I decided to lie on them. It was uncomfortable but at least I wasn't causing a security alert by leaving my bag unattended. As I drifted off, I could have sworn the tannoy was requesting David Bowie to report to the information desk. Surely not?

Mid-afternoon. I awoke with a start. Dreams inspired by the terrifying sound effects of the adjacent arcade machine had made sleep, shall we say, fitful. The paranoia of the public sleeper had set in. Had my pockets been picked? Had I been snoring, farting or dribbling? Maybe I'd had an erection. Certainly all the surrounding seats were strangely empty and no one was playing the machine. Probably the explanation was they they'd all caught their bloody planes and I hadn't.

People watching was bringing negative rewards. Fat, ugly, middle-aged blokes had ravishing beauties on their arms. The old Joe Jackson song "Is She Really Going Out With Him?" came to mind. Maybe it was a hallucination based on the article about Russian brides I'd been reading. Whatever could I find to do? Maybe I needed some knickers after all. My idea of excitement had been reduced to seeing if Garfunkels sold cups of tea.

And then, another thought: Maybe there'd been an announcement while I was asleep? How was I to find out? Swordfish Airways' desk was deserted and their VDU merely said "Position Closed". The travel agent's desk had an even odder sign: "Manned two hours before departure." When the heck was that going to be? And why hadn't it said "personned"?

Ah! An update. Old Sweaty-Brow informed us he'd personally put the wheel on a flight to Lyon (no wonder his brow was sweaty). Sadly, that flight had, in turn, been delayed and the earliest possible departure time for us would be 7.30 pm. I decided to give up and go home but changed my mind when told I wouldn't get any compensation until the delay had reached twelve hours (which would have been at 11.45 pm).

Interesting news: Garfunkels do serve tea, so I decided to blow the entire refreshment voucher on an "All Day Breakfast". I had, after all, just woken up.

"Enjoy your meal."

"Thank you."

"You're welcome."

"Oh, excuse me. The menu says 'fried potatoes' and these are hash browns."

"I'm sorry, sir. I'll get you some fried potatoes."

"Thank you."

"You're welcome."(Short pause).

"Excuse me, the menu says 'fried potatoes' and these are chips."

"Chips are fried potatoes, sir."

"No, chips are chips. I want fried potatoes."

"I'm sorry, sir, but we don't serve fried potatoes."

"But the menu says... Oh well, I'll have the chips."

"You're welcome."

"Say that again and I'll smash your face in."

The last sentence remained unspoken, but the relaxation exercises had definitely worn off. Gatwick Airport is a gigantic Cinemascope version of Fawlty Towers. Seven cups of tea later, the announcement came:

"My aircraft" - (Sweaty Brow seemed to think he owned it) - "has left Lyon and will get here ... er ... eventually. Await further announcements."

My bladder was swishing with tea but I was scared of losing my place and the machine-gun toting policemen would certainly blow up my bag if I left it in Garfunkels. Gritting of the teeth ensued and the relaxation exercises were recommenced.

It was 7.30 pm and still no sign of any action. Suddenly, I was starting to get both worried and annoyed. If I couldn't be sure of finding somewhere to stay in Madrid (it was now inevitable that we were going to arrive late at night), I wasn't going to go. Even if it meant losing the money I'd spent on the ticket, I wasn't prepared to risk having to walk the streets all night. It was also getting near to the time when it would be too late for me to catch a train home. I desperately needed information and advice, but no one anywhere was able to offer either. What had started out as a bit of a laugh had become thoroughly unpleasant.

At 7.45 pm I made a decision and burned my boats by finally entering the Departure Lounge. There was old Sweaty Brow, valiantly fending off the flak from the increasingly Dunkirk-spirited passengers. His tactic was to dole out business cards and invite people to write letters of complaint (*déjà vu*, and not that long ago either). Estimated departure time was now 9.30 pm, estimated arrival 1 am, likelihood of finding a hotel: debatable. I met the nicest and most coherent person I'd encountered all day, a cleaning lady who offered sympathy and polished the pot plants with her mop.

The plane, rather sweetly called "Katie", left at 1.45 am and arrived in Madrid shortly after 3.30 am. Everywhere was closed, so I used my newly-acquired sleeping at airports skills and managed to make it through to the morning alive.

In the morning, having decided to head for Granada, I had to do something about getting from the airport to the train station, in order to get the Euro Domino rolling. (Yes, I know dominoes can't roll, but too bad). The man at the enquiry office said that one could take a taxi but that the metro would be cheaper. The only problem was that it would involve five changes. What? Surely not? On the metro map, it looked no distance at all. The clerk took out a biro and traced the route, like one of those maze puzzles you find in magazines.

Some metro systems operate on destinations (Paris), others on numbers (Frankfurt) and yet others on colours (London). Madrid's metro seemed to operate on all three, so I sat on my suitcase and wrote out a precise itinerary. Feeling quite proud of this, I started to lug my suitcase down the first of a sod's law-style series of out-of-order escalators. The first four changes were so gratifyingly smooth that I stupidly began to feel quite smug. Almost blasé, in fact, until, on the last link, I suddenly became aware that the names of some of the stations were rather familiar. We seemed to be going back along the route we had just taken.

Baffled, I leapt out at the next stop and wondered what to do. A small notice on the wall caught my eye: *Trabajos*. It appeared that, because of work on the line, the metro simply stopped half way along and set off back the way it had come. Anyone wishing to continue in the same direction had to descend, struggle up to a bus (the first of which helpfully slammed its door in my face and drove off), travel two stops on the bus, get off again and plunge back into the metro system for just one stop. This operation, what with all the traffic, road works, etc, took thirty minutes and could have been walked in ten.

The bus stop was outside a sports centre. The next day, I was absently watching the news on TV, when my eye was caught by a scene which seemed familiar yet somehow different. The report was telling me that the sports centre had been blown up by a Basque terrorist bomb later that day, killing several people. Shudder!

The next train to Granada wasn't going to be until mid-afternoon and wouldn't arrive until nearly midnight. I started to worry about finding somewhere to sleep, so, having ascertained that neither Tourist Information nor Hotel Reservations dealt with places outside of Madrid, I took out my trusty Rough Guide and decided to ring some Hostals in Granada. Should be easy enough, but wait, the phones only operated with phone cards. Where did you get them? The Tourist Information man said there was a machine at the far end of the hall, so off I set. Damn, *"Defecto"*. Back to Tourist Info. No problem, there's another machine at the opposite end of the hall. Rumble, rumble, squeak, squeak, went the increasingly rebellious wheels of the suitcase. Guess what, *"Defecto"*. Back to Tourist Info. Don't worry, they sell them at the Post Office. Where's that? Down the road somewhere.

At that stage, the luggage had to go. I followed the signs to the Left Luggage hall and passed my case and rucksack through the X-ray machine. The official in charge had a truncheon and a gun, and appeared to take pleasure in watching the foreign tourists struggling with the impenetrable system for actually making the lockers work. This involved using the correct change, which of course no one had, least of all the official, and punching in a secret number. Confusion reigned and tears of frustration flowed.

Down the road apiece, I found the post office, but didn't bother to enter it, as even a Spanish dunce like me could tell that the huge posters in the window showing a phone card with a cross through it demonstrated that they most certainly did not sell phone cards. Luckily, I spotted a sign saying, helpfully, *"Telefonos"*, and bought a card from a nice man in a shop which seemed to sell nothing else. If I'd possessed the linguistic ability, I'd have recommended him to set up shop in the train station.

The Rough Guide listed a series of lovely-sounding Hostals in Granada. Phrase book at the ready, I dialled a series of numbers, all of which worryingly gave answers containing the word *"completo"*. Eventually, though, I was convinced that I had found one with space, and was certain that I'd reserved a room and informed them that I wouldn't be arriving until around midnight.

So it was with a light heart that I boarded the sensationally comfortable train. It was practically empty, air-conditioned, with plenty of leg room, and the guard handed out personal headphones, just like on a plane. A TV monitor flickered into life and what looked like a Spanish soap started up. But, apart from the wooden acting, it had little in common with any mid-afternoon soap that I had come across before. Within a minute, a glamorous actress had sat astride a paralysed man in a wheelchair, whipped off her bra and was rubbing her breasts in his face. You never get that in "Crossroads". While I blushed and looked away, the few other passengers, including several young children, seemed completely unconcerned. But then they weren't British, were they?

My arrival in Granada was enlivened by my first ever encounter with Tourette's Syndrome. Nothing else could explain the behaviour of the Scotsman in front of me in the taxi queue. Addressing all his remarks to his rather cowed-looking wife, he just couldn't stop swearing:

"That fucking cunt just fucking jumped the queue," he said of a man who had been quite legitimately at the front of the queue all along. "I'll fucking kill him, the cunt."

When they reached the front of the queue, he seemed dissatisfied with the driver who had arrived:

"He won't fucking know where to go, he's a fat cunt."

It's hard to picture how they communicated their destination to the driver, because no phrase book I have ever come across covers this sort of vocabulary.

My taxi driver, worryingly, had never heard of the Hostal address I gave him on a piece of paper. It took a lengthy perusal of the map before he had enough confidence to drive off. But he spoke fluent English, French and German and was immensely proud of his town.

"After a day in Granada, you will wish you could stay for a week," he announced.

Then, a few minutes later, he changed his mind:

"After a day in Granada, you will wish you could stay for a month."

And, as he deposited me at the end of a dark alley that looked an unlikely place to find a Hostal, he made his final pronouncement:

"After a day in Granada, you will wish you could stay for ever!"

My priority, however, was to sleep for ever, and to that end, I entered a tiny, creaking lift to the fourth floor, where a small sign told me the Hostal would be. Repeated ringing of the bell elicited a little old lady in a night dress, who showed no sign of having any knowledge of my arrival (it had been a male voice on the phone). What little I understood of her included several renditions of the dreaded word *"completo"*.

Outside in the alley, I began to feel desperate. It had been bad enough staying up all night or sleeping on park benches as a young student, but I was, for Christ's sake, approaching my 53rd birthday. So the last thing I needed was a dodgy-looking young man approaching me. Listen, I am fed up with being frightened by people in dark alleys, right?

Except that Manolo, as he introduced himself, wasn't at all frightening. In perfect English, he explained that he and his wife had a Hostal with a room free, just round the corner. And so it transpired, a lovely, spotless, beautifully decorated Hostal with a sitting room and dining room I could use whenever I wanted. Manolo and his wife couldn't have been more helpful and made my stay in Granada, while perhaps not quite as ecstatic as the taxi driver had predicted, a real pleasure.

It was in Granada that the Euro Domino Achilles heel began to show itself again. I had a brilliant idea which entailed going back to Madrid via Ronda and Seville. According to the map, it was a perfectly feasible route, but the problem was that, far from being able to hop, free of care, onto the train, I knew from the French experience that the ticket I had was no use without a reservation. And to get a reservation, you had to join the ticket-buying queue, which meant you actually had no advantage at all.

But even to find this out involved a trek which took up almost an entire day. First, I approached Tourist Information, which took an age to find. Ah no, they had no train information, but any travel agent would arrange reservations for me. The first travel agent said he couldn't, but maybe another one could. The next one was full and so was the one after that. The final one had a nice lady who gave me lots of train times (out of date and wrong, as it turned out), but couldn't carry out the reservations. For that, I would have to go to the train station.

This took over an hour, down a busy by-pass, only slightly enlivened by passing the house of the poet Federico García Lorca. At the station, the fun began. The man in the enquiry office took pride in telling me that the only language he spoke, other than Spanish, was Catalan. Yes, I know it's shameful that I don't speak Spanish, but in a city crammed with American and Japanese tourists, you'd think they'd make the teeniest effort, surely, to ensure that their employees could communicate with the clients?

With difficulty, I managed to convey that I wanted to go from Seville to Madrid on the following Sunday (almost a week away). This would be no problem, was the reply. Silence. Right, can I make a reservation? Yes. Silence. Okay, can I do that, please? Oh no, that was the responsibility of another part of the station, the ticket office. Couldn't he do it? Certainly not. This was the enquiry office, which answered enquiries. Silly of me.

Oh well, never mind. It couldn't be that difficult, could it? Yes, it could. As I attempted to join the queue at the ticket office, I realised that it wasn't, in fact, a queue as we know it. Although the people were standing in line, they had, in fact, plucked tickets from an obscurely placed machine and were waiting, just like at the deli counter at Asda, for their number to appear on an illuminated display board. Reasonable, I suppose ... except that my number was 942 and the number on the display board was 615. Bloody hell! No wonder the hall was full of worried-looking people glancing at their watches.

But there was method in this madness. The method was to get rid of any time-wasters, who would give up and go away. Of the five windows, only two were occupied, both by surly-looking, chain-smoking people who shook their heads dolefully in response to anything the customers asked (mainly "Do you speak English / German / French / Japanese?"). The moment one transaction was dealt with, the clerk pressed the button to move on to the next number. If no one was at the counter within five seconds (I exaggerate not), the next number went up, then the next, and then the next. If you missed it, tough luck, you had to get a new number, probably another hour away.

So I concentrated hard and - feeling severely intimidated by the whole procedure - wrote down my entire enquiry on a piece of paper to hold up in front of the window. It was in impeccable Spanish; after all, there had been plenty of time to consult the phrase book.

Hmm. Click click click went the ancient computer keys. Shake shake shake went the head. Whatever I wanted was impossible. There was absolutely no way I could get from Seville to Madrid. *Completo, Completo.* Christ! I'd never get home. What the taxi driver had meant wasn't that you'd want to stay for ever, but that you'd have to. Er ... okay, what if I stay here and go direct to Madrid? Click click click ... *Si*, at six o'clock in the morning, only two spaces left. Yes, yes, book it now! *Si*, two thousand one hundred and twenty-five pesetas supplement. *Qué?* But look, I've got a Euro Domino pass. Sorry, the supplement is still payable.

Imagine trying to communicate 2125 pesetas on your fingers and convey a look of surprise at the same time. That's what I did. The clerk took another drag on her cigarette, shrugged her shoulders and said take it or leave it. I took it. What choice was there? It wasn't until I had stepped away from the counter and allowed the next customer to submit himself to the ritual humiliation that I realised something else. The next door clerk had his microphone switched on, so loud, in fact, that the whole station could hear what he was saying. But mine hadn't switched hers on at all, which made her even more difficult to understand. Had I maybe misunderstood the extra fee? After all, the supplement on the way down had been just 400 pesetas. But no, there it was in black and white on the ticket: 2125 pesetas. I put it down to it being a Sunday.

That evening, I compared notes with a Texan backpacker who had booked onto the same train, the same day, for the same journey on the same type of ticket. Guess what? Her supplement had only cost 400 pesetas. So, much as I suspected, the sour-faced clerk was making the prices up, depending on what she thought about each customer.

So beware of the Euro Domino in Spain. Far from swanning straight on to your train, you'll still have to stand in queues and you'll still have to dip into your pocket. As for God, I don't think much of him if his good Catholic followers use Sunday as an excuse to charge you five times more than the usual fee. You'd think he'd do something about it.

I got some great photos of various exciting items of fruit and veg (plus lots of funny looks), and also discovered Ronda, surely one of the most beautiful towns in the whole of Europe. Half the town is called San Francisco, that should give you a clue. This was where Ernest Hemingway based much of "For Whom The Bell Tolls", with the result that they named a street after him. Hey, this means I have something in common with Ernest Hemingway. That's writing something in Ronda, not having a street named after me.

In Ronda, I checked into the "Hostal Colón", which offered *en suite* rooms at 3000 pesetas a night, which I worked out to be about £12. There was an immediate crisis when I ordered a cheese toasted sandwich. In a scene spookily reminiscent of the Rothenburg ob der Tauber débacle, the sandwich came complete with lumps of ham. When I requested a sandwich without ham, the waitress merely removed the meat and returned the sandwich. I watched her do it, she watched me watching her do it, and still she did it.

I did, however, forgive the Hostal Colón. When, after three days, I asked them to tot up all the various breakfasts, teas, sandwiches, mineral waters and beers I had accumulated, they waved me away, declaring that everything was *"inclusivo"*. Now that's my type of hotel!

Back at Madrid airport, things were not looking beautiful at all. The return flight was cancelled altogether and I was put on a plane for Cardiff. A coach then took me and another hapless victim (yes, an entire coach for two people) to Gatwick, arriving at 1.15 am. The first train home was at 5.38 am, which meant that I had to spend the night attempting to sleep, like a tramp, on the same bloody seat next to the same bloody gaming machine, a scarf wrapped round my head to try and keep out the glaring light. Following this came - you guessed - a lengthy sojourn at a sodden Clapham Junction.

That added an appropriate air of symmetry to the Domino, a bit like a double six.

For whom the sandwich tolls.

Chapter 9
Canal Treatment

And so the never-ending search continued for a Conventional Family Holiday that all of us would enjoy. Boating had been dismissed as an option because everybody in the family except me gets seasick in the bath (so they have showers instead). And yet ... there was something about canal narrowboats which suggested that they might provide the solution. After all, there are no waves on canals. So we started to look through canal holiday brochures.

Part of the appeal of a narrowboat is that it has absolutely everything a normal home would have, but in miniature. It's almost like playing with a doll's hose, it's so dinky and cosy. It absolutely appeals to my womb complex because you feel so safe and enclosed.

You get the same effect in caravans and mobile homes. Although we all hate the travelling ones clogging up the roads and swinging about dangerously in front of us, and everyone agrees that there are few things more ugly and ecologically reprehensible than a sprawling coastal caravan park, the fact is that, when you're in one, you feel great. You've got your diddy little bijou kitchenette, your tiny little loo, your almost luxurious sofas and your pretend kingsize bed, but everything is tiny, just like a Polly Pocket. And in the winter, it's even better. You can turn up your flame effect gas fire, put the kettle on and pretend you're in a kangaroo's pouch.

Everything you've got in a caravan, with the possible exception of the flame effect gas fire, you've got on a narrowboat, except that everything is - er - well, narrower. There's a sweet little TV that never works because canals are invariably in poor reception areas, the shower actually doubles as the loo (you can do both at the same time, if the fancy takes you), and of course there's a tiny fridge for your beer and a galley table that, after you have had supper and played cards on it, conveniently turns itself into a second double bed. So, against the odds, even a small narrowboat will sleep four people. Perfect for a Conventional Family Holiday, in fact.

We chose the Monmouth and Brecon canal because it was classified as ideal for beginners. With a maximum speed of 3 mph and not too many locks, said the brochure, it "winds through stunningly beautiful countryside and remote country villages". And it was all true. All my memories of that first canal holiday are of wonderful, relaxing times and pleasant experiences.

Well, maybe apart from the first night and the second morning (or the first morning, if you see what I mean, because take-over time on canal boats tends to be late afternoon). The advance details had assured us that we would receive comprehensive training in how to handle the boat, but what we got didn't precisely fit that description. A nice man steered us out of the boatyard, a few yards down the canal as far as the first bridge, said, "Okay, it's this way for forward and this way for reverse", hopped off onto the towpath and strolled back towards whence he had come.

"Hey, what about the instructions? Oh Christ, how do we open the bridges? How do we get through the locks?" I called after him, plaintively.

"Don't worry," his reply wafted back. "There's a book in the cabin. It'll tell you all you need to know."

As probably every beginner does, we travelled until the first drawbridge hove into sight, steered carefully into the bank (literally into it), bashed in the two iron pegs provided and tied up to them, before getting out the book and studying it in uncomprehending detail.

We had not the slightest idea what a lock was, what it did, or how it functioned. We certainly had no inkling of how much strength, energy, skill and courage it would require to get through one. But that was still to come. For the time being, we stayed put, cooked some tinned ravioli (the staple diet of campers everywhere) and snuggled down for the night. The rain hammered on the steel roof (narrowboats are made entirely of steel), making it seem even cosier.

We were rudely, very rudely awakened at 7 am. The children, who must have been about seven and ten years old, came screaming into our cabin from their little room at the front (oh bloody hell, all right, the bows) of the boat:

"Mummy, Daddy, help, help!"

(Yawn). "Whatever is the matter?"

"There's a wolf!"

"Don't be silly, what do you mean?"

"There's a wolf on the boat!"

"I'm sure there aren't any wolves in Wales. Now go back to sleep and leave us in peace."

"No, no, there really is a wolf."

Too much late-night reading and a vivid imagination, I thought, but that didn't explain why both girls had the same story. What had happened, they said, was that they had heard some scrabbling, scratching and panting at their window, opened the curtains and been confronted by, well, a wolf, leering through the window at them and baring its teeth. They were genuinely terrified.

We were, as one almost always is on a narrowboat, absolutely in the middle of nowhere, in some dense woods and several miles from any houses. You hear tales of panthers in Somerset, so why not a wolf in the Brecon Beacons? I decided to proceed with extreme caution and tweaked the curtains.

"Aaargh! There IS a wolf!"

"Na nee na nee poo poo, told you so, Dad!"

Sitting on the prow of our boat and peering in was a grey coloured creature, emaciated and severely bedraggled from the rain. After I had recovered from the initial shock, I plucked up courage to look again. It obviously wasn't a wolf (shame), but it was a dog, a mongrellish-looking thing with sad eyes and a lolling tongue. What on earth were we to do?

I certainly wasn't going to dare to approach it, for fear of having my hand snapped off, but Birgit, practical as ever, declared, "It's probably hungry", opened the door ("No, no, it'll eat us!") and tossed out a slice of Mother's Pride, which the creature wolfed (sorry) down in a millisecond. So out went another slice and, before we knew it, most of the loaf was gone.

As the dog breakfasted, we had a chance to observe its body language. Despite its scruffiness, there was something distinctly friendly about it. It was pretty clear that, far from being a wild, rabid Hound From Hell, it was simply lost and was seeking our company. By half past eight, we were stroking and petting it and the children were demanding that we should adopt it and take it home.

Someone spotted that it had a collar with one of those little screw-top containers attached to it. I opened it and inside, there was a piece of paper with a name, "Guto", and a phone number. This was one affectionate creature, in fact the nicest dog any of us had ever met, and it had decided to adopt us (rather than the other way round). This was the canine version of the adage, so often proved in this book, that you should never judge or condemn a person (or an animal) on first appearances.

"What we'll have to do," I said, "is cruise on to Pencelli" - the next village - "and phone the owners. Then they can come and pick him up."

"Aaaw, can't we keep him?"

"No, that wouldn't be fair on his owners, would it?" I said, sanctimoniously (although I'd have been quite keen to take him home myself).

The instruction book contained copious details about the checking and greasing that needed to be carried out on the engine before starting up each day, so it was a while before I could switch on the engine. We cooked some bacon (most of which was eaten by Guto) and then the moment came. I turned the key and the engine spluttered into life. Now that may seem a cliché, but engines always splutter into life, and this one was no exception. And that was it. Guto was gone. He jumped about six feet in the air, launched himself off the edge of the boat, dived headlong into the undergrowth and disappeared.

"Aaaw, now look what you've done. You scared him."

"Well, I didn't know he'd be scared, did I?"

"But now ..." (kind of a sob) ... "we'll never see Guto again."

Half an hour's worth of searching in the woods and much calling of "Guto! Guto!" later, we had to admit that he was gone. But we did still have the piece of paper with the phone number on it. So when we got to Pencelli, I found a phone box and dialled the number.

What's the time, Mr Wolf?

The man at the other end of the line was absolutely flabbergasted. The story had gone as follows: Guto was a much-loved family pet in Cardiff, many miles away. Two weeks earlier, he had been out walking with his family in the country when someone let off a shotgun nearby. Guto, a nervous creature, completely freaked, took off in terror and, despite much whistling and calling, and repeated visits to the area over the following few days, hadn't been seen again.

The owner had, by now, given up hope, so was naturally amazed and thrilled by my call. If Guto had been on the run for so long, and for such a great distance, no wonder he was in such a state. And if he was nervous, no wonder he had bolted as soon as we made a loud noise. I had to tell the owner that, although we could tell him roughly where Guto was, we didn't actually have him in our possession. That was how we left it, except that Birgit had the brainwave of putting a notice in the local shop, detailing

Guto's tale (that's tale, not tail) and giving the number of his owners.

A week later, we received a letter from Guto's master. Some SAS soldiers on an exercise had found Guto in the woods, seen our notice, put two and two together and rung him up in Cardiff. In his letter, he told us Guto's life story (far from being a mongrel, he was some kind of pedigree breed) and even enclosed a tenner to buy a little something for the girls. He had found out our address through detective work and locating the boatyard, so he must have been genuinely thrilled to have Guto back where he belonged.

So our first narrowboat holiday had got off to an exciting start, and every other aspect of it was an unmitigated pleasure, too. The Monmouth and Brecon Canal was as scenic as the brochure had promised. It was extremely narrow and also only a couple of feet deep, so we frequently ran aground. At first, this induced panic, but we soon found that a gentle push-off with a wooden pole got you back on track.

One of the reasons the Monmouth and Brecon was such a good starting point for the inexperienced was that it had a bit of everything, but nothing in excess. For example, there were several drawbridges (operated by a winch) and also quite a long tunnel, into which the boat only just fitted. The steerer had to crouch down behind the cabin with just enough head room to peer over the top at the white dot in the distance, which took a long time to get closer, as the maximum speed in the tunnel was 1 mile an hour. You had to switch on the headlights and hoot occasionally to make sure that no one was daft enough to enter the other end on a collision course.

There are few pleasures greater that tying up outside a canalside pub and nipping in for a Guinness. Of course, we did this on several occasions, but another attraction of the "Mon and Brec" (as it allows friends like us to call it) is that you can walk into a number of attractive small towns and villages for pub suppers. We tried out Abergavenny, Crickhowell and Brecon itself, all of them delightful places. On each occasion, during the torchlit walk back to the boat, we resurrected a tradition first piloted all those years before, hitch-hiking with Martin: riotous games of Twenty Questions. The best clue Lucy and I ever came up with was the piece of paper with Guto's name on it (*Vegetable*: paper and *Mineral*: ink). And the sods got it on the twentieth question.

What's that you say? The locks? Oh, all right. There was no getting away from them. If you avoid facing up to locks, you're not going to get very far. Some canals have hundreds and hundreds of the damn things. As soon as you leave one, you can see the next bastard approaching, or, even worse, you get involved in a "flight" of locks, where you move from one straight into another and sometimes take a whole day to get up the side of a hill. The reason you have locks is that water doesn't flow uphill, but canals, which have no "flow" like a river, frequently go up and down hills which crop up en route; after all, they were the motorways of their day.

So, pay attention: Here, in case you ever need it, is what you need to do in order to get through a lock. For added clarity, remember that the gates are the massive wooden things that hold the water back and the paddles (an annoyingly misleading word) are the square-shaped pieces of metal that you winch open in order to allow the water to pour through the apertures in the shut gates. Lost you already, haven't I? Oh, and canal convention decrees that the bottom gates are always left open, allowing whoever is going upwards to drive straight in.

Going up (ladies' underwear, soft furnishings, oh, shut up):

1. Drop crew on bank.
2. Drive in (this was always Birgit's job, as she's a better driver).
3. Close the bottom gates and check that the paddles are down (i.e. closed).
4. Open the top paddles, allowing the water to flow in.
5. When the lock is full, open the top gate.
6. Drive out and hang about.
7. Close the top gate.

8. Wind down the top paddles.

9. Open the bottom paddles, allowing the water to flow out again.

10. When the lock is empty, open the bottom gates again.

11. Close the bottom paddles.

12. Crew charges along bank and rejoins the boat.

Going down (no, no, not that kind of going down):

I can't be bothered to write all that down, but it's vaguely the same in reverse.

Is this clear? I only ask, because this is my patented "simple" version of what to do. The instruction book was poorly laid out and expressed in mercilessly complicated language. It was also contained in a ring binder whose pages blew about in the wind as I scrabbled with it on the bank, frantically shouting instructions at my uncomprehending family. I therefore had the brilliant idea of distilling the instructions and putting them on to a laminated card. I sent this to the boatyard, but the sods never replied. I fully intend to return one day, to see whether they adopted it.

The entire locking process is, of course, accompanied by much monkey-like clambering about across the gates, winding of winches, pushing and pulling of gates and gesticulating with the heavy iron lock keys, which you inevitably either leave behind or drop into the deep water. And locks are deep, very deep indeed. And inhabited by vicious swirling currents. And while you're rushing about, there are all manner of bollards and other obstructions in your way.

Locks are dangerous. Apart from the likelihood of getting your limbs trapped in the various bits of machinery, there are three ways in which you could get into terrible trouble. The first would be tripping headlong and plunging into the water, hitting your head on the way. The second would be to forget to untie the ropes securing you to the bollards by the lock as it empties. If both ropes are attached, the entire boat will be left dangling in mid air, but if only one is attached, the boat will end up tipped at an angle with the crew slithering into the water. Or, worst of all, if you are too close to the front of the lock when the top paddles are opened and the water gushes out, the boat could simply fill with water and sink. All of these things have happened in the past and will no doubt happen in the future.

That's just by way of saying that locks are a serious business. If you take your children on a canal holiday, they need to be quite well behaved and pretty quick-witted. Which is another good reason for starting on the Mon and Brec (as we, its friends, are still allowed to call it), because its locks are fairly innocuous and not particularly deep.

One of the best things about canals is that they allow you to see the world from a different viewpoint. It's perfectly possible to cruise through Birmingham, say, or even London (try the Regent's Canal from Camden Lock), experiencing the cities, as it were, from behind, and getting little feeling of the pandemonium which is going on in the streets only a matter of yards away. That is why we have had fantastic canal holidays starting in Chelmsford ("Chelmsford? Why the bloody hell do you want to go to Chelmsford?") and even, come on, you've got to be joking, Basingstoke.

***

Life is full of preconceptions and one of them is that taking a holiday in Basingstoke is not a good idea. This is true. But what is also true is that the Basingstoke Canal isn't actually very near Basingstoke.

Another preconception is that canal holidays entail lots of very hard work. This is true as well, and I have the hernia to prove it. But what is also true is that the Basingstoke Canal enjoys 22 miles in which there is but one lock, surely a record. As we cruised in blistering sunshine and with the minimum of exertion, the *Observer* published what claimed to be a comprehensive guide to the navigable waterways of the UK and failed even to mention the existence of the Basingstoke Canal. Meanwhile, the leaflet from the Canal Centre described it as the country's most beautiful waterway. Curiouser and curiouser.

The truth was that, as we discovered, the Basingstoke Canal offers an oasis of tranquillity that paradoxically manages to travel through military establishments, shooting ranges and large suburban conurbations, while completely ignoring all of them. At the same time, we were gaining unique access to nature reserves, unspoilt countryside and historical sites, virtually without leaving home. This time, we reasoned, nothing could go wrong.

Yeah, well. Here's how our particular catalogue of disasters went. After a first day of unparalleled tranquillity, we tied up at the Swan pub in Ash Vale. Click, went the padlock on the door as we departed, salivating in preparation for our pub meal. Click, went my brain, as I realised sickeningly - shit - that the key to the padlock was still inside the cabin.

This posed a severe problem, since it was impossible to get into the boat any other way and the folder containing the emergency number of the boatyard was securely locked inside as well. As a night spent sleeping on the towpath didn't appeal, I had no alternative but to take the children's gleeful advice and perpetrate some advanced vandalism in the form of snapping the padlock apart with the help of the thoughtfully-provided boathook. Um, in fact it had been thoughtfully provided for a different purpose. Still, effective as this action was, it did induce a certain amount of anxiety as to the padlock's usefulness as an anti-burglary device.

In the morning, some friends arrived for a quiet day's cruising. Within minutes of starting off, one of them tried out the loo but fell foul of a flaw in the flushing device. Amid much screaming, it was ascertained that the toilet was overflowing and rapidly flooding the main cabin. Hurtling below to try to give assistance, I thrust the tiller into the hands of the other visitor, omitting to remember that he had never steered a boat before. It was only seconds before we had veered into a strictly prohibited nature reserve, narrowly missing the nest of some rare aquatic bird and necessitating a very complicated and tortuous manoeuvre to get ourselves facing back in the right direction. After this, Lucy's complaint that she had dropped her sunglasses into the water hardly even registered.

That evening, we decided (well, of course we did) on a pub meal. As much of the canal wanders hesitantly through the built-up areas of Fleet, Farnborough and Aldershot, most of the pubs turned out to be chains and the only one which wasn't, expressed astonishment at our request for food. I thought that the question was fairly reasonable in view of the fact that there was a large sign outside declaring "Pub Food".

All turned out for the best, since Fleet boasts the most fantastic Nepalese restaurant, where the food and standards of service were some of the best any of us had ever encountered. Returning to the boat, we noticed a larger than usual proportion of completely legless youths emerging from the many "over-18s only" theme pubs and briefly wondered whether we had been wise to moor so close to the town centre. This suspicion was substantiated when we awoke next morning to discover that we had been cast adrift in the night. Not that a canal is an environment where any water-hog is likely to zoom round the corner and crash into you, but it was disconcerting nonetheless.

Even more disconcerting was the news in the Sunday paper. Some maniac had been constructing nail bombs and planting them in areas where he hoped to inflict damage on minorities which he had taken against, such as black people or gays. His latest atrocity had been to plant a bomb in a gay pub in Soho, killing and injuring a number of innocent people. Now, we were being asked to believe, he had finally been arrested at his bomb factory, a seemingly innocuous semi-detached house not half a mile from where we were moored. No wonder our sleep had been disturbed by an unusually large number of police sirens. Okay, so of course we hadn't been in any kind of danger, but it was kind of disturbing to think that such evil could lurk so close to our tranquillity. Moral: Don't buy the Sunday papers.

Still, any canal holiday will have its adventures and, to be frank, it would be slightly disappointing if all you did was cruise gently along doing nothing else. The Basingstoke Canal did allow for much gentle cruising, especially as there were so few interruptions. The sole lock was at Ash Vale and there were only a couple of swing bridges. If we had attempted to progress all the way to Byfleet, there would have been a little matter of a further 39 locks, but we would have needed several weeks and special permission to attempt that (and also to have been clinically insane).

What we did was to set off initially westwards from the boatyard near Odiham, where we hired the boat, and we easily reached Mytchett, where the so-called Deep Cut flight of locks began. In the three available days, we had plenty of time to turn and retrace our route and also follow the canal eastwards to the limit of its navigability, which is the now-blocked Greywell tunnel, home to many bats, including some rare species. Nearby we found Odiham Castle, built in 1207 and known as King John's Castle, after he fled there from his barons in 1215, before riding on to Runnymede to sign the Magna Carta. This monument is that rare entity, a castle which has no kiosk demanding an admission fee. We were free to wander at liberty.

There, that was informative, wasn't it?

The parts of the canal around Odiham are entirely rural, with many opportunities to study wildlife in the form of coots, moorhens, swans, herons and their fluffy offspring. Even in the areas around Aldershot, where we were travelling through military land and housing estates, there were many large expanses of open water, known as "flashes", which are managed as nature reserves. Indeed, as is usual on canals, we were transported into a kind of parallel world in which you are part of the familiar environment yet somehow strangely detached from it.

So it wasn't a misprint. Basingstoke, honest.

The following year, we thought we'd try out the Kennet and Avon Canal, which came highly recommended as particularly rewarding. We started in Aldermaston (ulp - was the water radioactive?) and cruised through Hungerford and Newbury. In general, we found things a bit more taxing than in the past, in that there were masses of locks and a few weirs with strong currents. But the week was notable for two contrasting things. Firstly, we actually got stuck, one evening, in a deserted lock when the mechanism jammed, and had to be rescued by the Waterways Board (a bit like the AA in a boat); and secondly, the girls got to meet Ruby Wax, whom they inexplicably (but it's true, I promise) found playing football with some kids in a field in Little Bedwyn. Don't ask.

***

By far our greatest canal adventure came in the most unlikely of locations and in the most unfortunate of circumstances. We'd had such fun on canal holidays that we had invited some friends to join us, with their children, on what promised to be perhaps a slightly more sociable event than the earlier canal trips.

It didn't turn out that way. As we arrived at the boatyard, the owner was waiting for us.

"Your friends phoned to say they aren't coming."

"What? Why ever not?"

"They say you should phone them."

To cut it short, their marriage had collapsed. The night before, they had had a showdown about a range of issues which meant that spending a week cooped up in the confines of a narrowboat (not to mention being jolly with us) was completely out of the question. Sorry, mates, you're on your own.

This was a bit of a shock, but there was a bigger shock to come. It turned out that we weren't anywhere near where I had thought we would be. The canal I had selected from the catalogue had been the picturesque, rural Leeds and Liverpool Canal at Silsden, in the Yorkshire Dales, but we seemed to be in a bit of an industrial wasteland. What had gone wrong?

Only I could do this. (Yes, only you could do this, agreed the family, accusingly and not at all impressed). Not only had I quoted the wrong reference number from the wrong page of the brochure, but I hadn't even noticed, naively just following the directions thoughtfully provided by the hire firm and not realising they were taking us nowhere near Silsden. Where were we? In Mirfield, West Yorkshire. Never heard of it? Exactly.

But there was a silver lining. On the useless little TV in the cabin, despite the rice pudding on the screen, we could hear Michael Fish loud and clear: "Cool and wet over Spain and the Mediterranean." We, however, almost immediately found ourselves lavishly applying the sunscreen and stretching luxuriously on the sweltering roof of the good ship "Helen". Where? Why, on the Rochdale canal, of course. Here we go again with that old "ignore your preconceptions" adage.

The first few hours after leaving the base almost decided us to knock the project on the head completely. Aside from entailing a lengthy series of very difficult manoeuvres through flood locks on and off the river, the Calder and Hebble Navigation made its way through a less-than inviting landscape of tatty industrial estates and wildly malodorous sewage works. It was uncomfortably near one of these waste processing plants that Lucy succeeded in slipping off the edge of the boat and into the Brown Windsor soup which masqueraded as water. Whilst heroically rescuing her (and planning my forthcoming appearance on "999"), I kept up an essential mantra: "For God's sake don't swallow anything."

Before long, however, things looked up a lot. We reached the in-the-process-of- being-lovingly- restored metropolis of Sowerby Bridge, where, the canal guide-book assured us, the canal would "retire into a telephone box and emerge wearing its underpants outside its tights". And blow me, it did, in pretty spectacular fashion.

First, again from the trusty guide book, we had time to take on board the warning that this was one of the most difficult stretches of canal in the country. Well, great. There we were, a family featuring a prize wimp (me), a well-disposed but frankly not very muscular wife and two keen but small daughters. Our sole previous criterion for canal selection had been to choose those which had the fewest locks. And the first thing which confronted us was only the deepest lock in the UK, that's all.

Luckily, there was a trusty lock-keeper to guide us through. His tactics were ideal: At first, he was strict and authoritarian, but by the time you emerged at the top (having obeyed all his orders to the letter), he had become a kind uncle, dispensing tips and witticisms by the gallon.

The locks on the Calder and Hebble and the Rochdale were like no others. First, you needed a normal lock key. Then you needed another type of lock key. And then it got difficult: You needed a whopping great baseball bat-like hunk of wood to open the top paddles of most of the Calder and Hebble ones (apparently unique in the country, and certainly worthy of the instruction course we received before setting off). And then, on the Rochdale, the most nerve-wracking of all: A tiny key to open the security protection encasing the lock mechanism itself. I spent the whole time in terror of dropping the only one we had into the murky depths.

The aim of those attacking the Rochdale Canal was to reach the "Summit", which is effectively the top of the Pennines, to which this waterway improbably but successfully climbs. We soon discovered that our allotted week was not going to be sufficient to achieve this and that we should really have started from Sowerby Bridge. Oh well, no point in crying over spilt sludge. Instead, we resolved to get to Todmorden and hike the rest of the way.

To a family which is half-German, Todmorden is a frightening appellation, meaning, as it roughly does, "Death and Murder". The children were threatening not to get off the boat there at all, but as we arrived, there were some worryingly "Todmorden" things to deal with, mainly associated with the young teenagers of Lancashire. I had become disquieted when, after waving cheerfully to a group of young men on the towpath, I felt a substantially-sized stone whistling past, millimetres from my ear. I turned round, spotted several youths bending down to pick up further ammunition, and opened the throttle. Luckily, Helen had a good turn of speed, and I briefly didn't care about exceeding the limit.

It came as no surprise to learn that Todmorden was one of the venues chosen by Dr Harold Shipman to carry out his serial murders. Most appropriate.

The "baseball bat" locks had upper and lower paddles. Obviously, you had to open the lower ones first if you didn't wish to be flooded, but the crew of a passing boat told us a cautionary tale. They had accepted the kind offer of some passing youths to allow the crew to stay on board while the lads operated the lock for them. You've guessed it: The kids purposely opened the top paddles first, causing the water to flow into the boat and putting the travellers in fear of their lives.

It was thus with some trepidation that, on the return leg, we arrived at Brighouse, back on the Calder and Hebble. A dozen young lads were taking advantage of the aforementioned Mediterranean weather to leap in and out of the full lock (yuk, I should say in passing). As we chugged into the lock, one young man suddenly leapt onto the boat, knocking Birgit so that the throttle shot forward and we inflicted quite serious damage upon the front gates. In my more imaginative moments, I find myself thinking about what might have happened if we'd hit them hard enough to burst them open (which we nearly did). It's too frightening to contemplate, but let's just say, we'd have been unlikely to have lived to tell the tale.

The place we fell in love with was called Hebden Bridge. It was like a kind of permanent Glastonbury Festival. Everyone we met had a pony tail, tie-dye gear and a dog on a string, and the atmosphere was friendly and laid-back. Me, I couldn't believe I'd actually seen the Trades Club, one of the few places where the Sex Pistols played live (unless I'm mistaken, of course. The Email address for complaints is at the front of the book.)

The hippie with whom we shared a lock possessed two canal boats and claimed to own large stretches of the canal bank; no wonder he had a permanent smile. The really crazy thing was that he said that he lived in Bridport, hundreds of miles away in Dorset. We just thought he was high and imagining it, but not at all. Months later, I actually met him in Bridport and he and his wife got me so drunk on Stella Artois that I fell asleep in my sister's garden and dreamed I was being dive-bombed by Stukas.

And so to the attempt upon the "summit". We donned our

walking boots and felt rather smug about being able to overtake the few boats struggling up the lengthy series of (sometimes almost completely empty) locks. We assumed that we'd be rewarded by a delicious lunch when we got to the top ... except that we didn't know that everything thereabouts shuts on Tuesdays. Well, would you have?

There were three pubs and several shops, and all of them were closed. We literally ran to the Bird I' th' Hand, one and a half miles away, to be informed that they'd stopped serving. It took all our combined talents of turning on the pathos to make them relent. Oh please, we've come such a long way and we've heard so much about Northern hospitality. Oh, all right then, just this once. Baguette and chips, yum.

Which reminds me ... You wouldn't expect the Rochdale Canal to be a gourmet trail, but that's just where you'd be wrong. In Sowerby Bridge, we had an Indonesian feast of unrivalled deliciousness, climaxed by a coffee which appeared swathed in enough dry ice to rival a Pink Floyd live concert. You couldn't see across the room. Hebden Bridge had the most fantastic vegetarian restaurant in the universe. And, on the way back, we naturally did the best thing in the world you can possibly do: tie up outside a pub and be at the bar in three strides. This was at the Colliers Arms outside Elland.

This particular trip was all about memories. And memories are made of:

... Dobsons' wonderfully quaint sweetie factory in Elland, where we met a genuine Dobson, the children were in paradise and we bought pounds and pounds of excessively E-numbered indulgences. I have a horrible feeling that it's probably been closed down or modernised, it was just too authentic to survive. Anyone know?

... Such as the unstoppably loquacious artist in Sowerby Bridge, who told us his life story several times over and sold us the ultimate souvenir, a personalised print of the canal's history.

... Such as the lady in (where else?) Hebden Bridge who had three dogs with flower pots on their heads. Yes, that's three dogs with flower pots on their heads. But it was Hebden Bridge.

... Such as all the lovely friendly people we met and the cosy times on the boat, basking on the roof or snuggled up in the evening with a good book.

Birgit said the only thing wrong with the Rochdale Canal was that the locks were so frequent that she didn't get to finish reading her novel. Well, you have to take the rough with the smooth.

The best thing in the world you can possibly do ...

Chapter 10
A Friend Indeed

I've just invented a proverb: "A friend indeed is a friend with whom you can go on holiday and still remain friends." It's hardly pithy, I accept, but, as a proverb should be, it's a nugget of wisdom and truth. Ask anybody whether they have survived a family holiday taken together with another family, and their faces will cloud over. Oh dear, they will say ...

But my friend Paul is indeed, a friend in need, and together with our families (Paul, admittedly, with the odd change of wife here and there), we have survived not one, but two joint holidays. Here's how.

Paul's son Sam was at crawling age and Annabel was a toddler when the idea of going away together cropped up. It was very late to do anything about it, but I got the number of an agency which hired out *gîtes* in France. The concept is glorious: You rent a beautiful, rustic cottage, adorned with geraniums, cool on the inside, fully equipped and in idyllic country surroundings ... Yes, please, we'll have some of that, *merci beaucoup*.

The agency sent me something suspiciously unglossy. Already, on the phone, they had sounded doom-laden about our chances of getting anything at all at this late stage, but through the post came a dingy-looking photocopy of a photocopy, with some semi-legible text and illustrations which took the form of black blobs. All but one of them had been crossed out in felt-tip.

The one remaining *gîte* sounded really nice. I worked out that it had open fireplaces, several bedrooms and was on a farm near to a small town called Châteleaudren, in Brittany. It seemed absolutely ideal, so we booked it.

To get us there, Paul borrowed his father-in-law's car. Well, actually, it was a car belonging to his father-in-law's company, and therefore to be treated with the most gentle of kid gloves. That the car wasn't entirely suitable soon became clear. It was a tiny little Vauxhall Nova, to which Paul attached a roof rack for our various cases, buggies, travel cots and other accoutrements.

That was fine (as long as we didn't travel under any low bridges), but the conditions inside weren't.

Birgit gets car sick if she sits in the back of a vehicle, so she joined Paul in the front. It needs to be noted at this stage that she was also several months pregnant with Lucy, so would have been vomiting all the time anyway, without the assistance of the various sick-making elements which the holiday was to throw up (sorry). Anyway, in the back were Paul's wife, Ali, plus me, Annabel (in a child seat) and Sam (on Ali's lap). The conditions were agonisingly cramped and of course the children both dribbled, puked and dropped food and drink all over themselves and us. Well, that's what you expect. Serve us right for having unprotected sex in the first place.

Sam (who nowadays is a pretty normal sort of chap) was "going through a phase". This particular phase entailed him being relatively quiet for reasonable periods, but every now and then, he would, for no apparent reason, let out a blood-curdling yell at a volume which, considering his small frame, was physically impossible. Except that he did it:

"Wuuuuaaaaaaaarrrgh!"

And then one more for luck:

"Wuuuuaaaaaaaarrrgh!"

So startling was this (planned each time, seemingly, to coincide with my finally descending into some kind of minor nap) that it was sufficient to seriously threaten to perforate my eardrum, as well as making me jump high enough to bash my head on the car's ceiling. It was excruciating, and it went on for hours and hours and hours.

Châteleaudren, it turned out, was a heck of a long way from Le Havre. But we had to go via Le Havre because Paul worked for P & O and could thus get cheap tickets. Dusk was falling as we finally reached the *gîte*, but even in the gathering shadows, we could perceive that it wasn't precisely the rural idyll that we had anticipated. The building itself was across the yard from the farmhouse and had no garden (so bang went the idea of sunbathing on the luxuriant lawn). Our arrival was greeted with a cacophonous barking from several slavering, rabid-looking Alsatians which roamed, lead-less, around the yard. The children were traumatised before they'd even got out of the car, as these creatures reared up against the windows, scratching them with their paws and frothing against the glass.

Having been trapped in the car for several minutes (there being no sign of any humans), we were eventually released when the surly farmer appeared and rather reluctantly called off the Hounds From Hell. He showed no willingness to react to my gushingly fluent and well-prepared French words of greeting. In one way, this was a relief, because I'm always getting into trouble by plunging headlong into foreign language conversations that I turn out to be incapable of sustaining; on the other hand, it would have been quite nice if he had made some slight attempt at being vaguely welcoming.

As we entered the musty-smelling house, we all became aware that we had picked up something on our shoes as we had walked across the yard.

"What's that?" asked Ali. "Oh God, it's cow shit!"

"Ah," - here, as someone who had spent several youthful summers working on farms, I came into my own - "ah no, that's certainly not cow shit, it hasn't got the right consistency. No, it's definitely chicken shit, and, do you know ..." (sniff) "... I could swear there's a hint of pigshit in there as well."

Damned impressive, I thought, but the others were too busy scraping their shoes and retching (remember the morning sickness) to appreciate the skill involved in my diagnosis.

In the morning, the composition of the unlikely cocktail was confirmed. In the yard roamed both pigs and chickens, all crapping away to their hearts' content.

"Why didn't you tell us it was a bloody pig farm?" demanded Paul.

"I didn't know!" I replied, truthfully.

"Here, let's have a look at that brochure. If it doesn't say anything about it being a pig farm, I'm going to ask for a refund."

Oh dear. A reappraisal of the photocopy did, indeed, reveal, in tiny print, the legend *"Entreprise porcine"*. Not that I would necessarily have recognised this slightly estate agents' blurb rose-tinted bespectacled mode of description, but clearly, all the other potential clients had, which was no doubt the reason why it was the only *gîte* left without a felt-tip cross. We had literally been crapped on.

"Things will look better in the morning" is a really silly expression which is hardly ever accurate. In my experience, things invariably look considerably worse in the morning. As they did on the starship *"Entreprise porcine"*. As shit goes, it's the piggy version which receives the worse press, but the chicken variety is actually far more pungent. It attracted eager flies and other creepy-crawlies which didn't at all mind entering our house. There being no lawn, the children couldn't be let out, for fear of either being covered in crap or eaten alive either by mosquitoes or rabid Alsatians. Oh, happy hols.

Inside, the house was as filthy as the interior of an unswept chimney. Sam crawled around for a few moments and was instantly transformed into a Black and White Minstrel (without the White bit). Of course, he tried to put his hands in his mouth and didn't comprehend why he wasn't allowed to (his "Wuuuuaaaaaaaaarrrghs!" being in this case quite understandable). His clothes couldn't be washed as the hot water had broken down. The children had to be washed in the sink because there was no bath.

But we were British, mainly, and upper lips were stiffened. We would just have to make the best of it, wouldn't we? So off we set (it rained every day, by the way, but that goes without saying) to visit a selection of extremely boring small towns, seedy, run-down zoos and rip-off amusement parks. Both couples went out to dinner twice (leaving the others to babysit), but the local restaurant had a very limited menu consisting of various types of tough, fatty meat and bony fish so obscure that their names weren't even listed in the dictionary. You can't go wrong with French food. Yeah, that's what we had thought as well.

Paul and I half-heartedly drove into Châteleaudren for a beer in its sole café, but the local "lads" looked at us so threateningly when we put a coin on the edge of the pool table to indicate that we'd like a game, that we abandoned both the coin and our beer, escaping while the going was good.

There was another doubtful sporting activity to be enjoyed at the farm. The farmer's wife, occasionally to be seen in a smock, hanging out washing, never actually made contact with us, but her daughter did. Cross-eyed and capable only of grunting (a bit like something they keep in the attic in Hammer films), she appeared at the door of our *gîte* every morning, cradling a "*boule*" in each hand, leered at us and indicated that we should follow her to the weedy gravel patch which masqueraded as a *boules* terrain. We didn't know the rules and she was incapable of explaining them, so the only way we could know how the game had gone was to watch her reactions. If she giggled inanely, she had won, but if she burst into tears and ran back to the farmhouse shouting curses, she had lost. In the latter case, both mum and dad would glower psychotically at us from behind the curtains.

As if in sympathy for our predicament, my one remaining wisdom tooth decided to make its hitherto unnoticed presence felt. But this time, it did so with a genuine sense of vengeance for some unspecified but evil crime I must have perpetrated against it (possibly neglecting it for a lifetime, for a start). This was no normal toothache, such as that encountered in Luxembourg. Oh, no, this was cancer of the jaw. Yes, it was. Only that could explain the horrendous agony with which I was overwhelmed.

For two days, I lay in a darkened room. The bed was rock hard, the rain hammered on the shutters, the smell from the yard was appalling, but I cared only for my jaw. I consumed massive overdoses of paracetemol, listened to Birgit assuring me that cancer of the jaw didn't exist and that, even if it did, I didn't have it, and begged her to plunge a knife into my heart and put me out of this misery. Surely, death would be infinitely preferable to this torture.

Eventually, Birgit found a chemist, who gave her some

suppositories. For me, not for her. Having a wife who is willing to shove things up your arse can sometimes be an advantage, but she trained as a nurse and so is experienced in doing unspeakable things to people. It wasn't as awful as I feared it would be, but it did no good. When we managed to translate what it said in the small print on the box, we realised that it contained merely a minor dose of aspirin. I begged to be taken to a dentist, but I was the only one who spoke French, and therefore eventually had to arrange it myself.

There was no phone in the *gîte* (laughable notion), so enquiries had to be made from a rural phone box without the help of any Yellow Pages, not an easy thing to do when you can open your mouth no more than a millimetre wide. No doubt our hosts could have helped, but the farmer was permanently out and his wife pretended to be.

I won't go into detail about what the village dentist did. Oh, all right then, I will. Diagnosing that there was a reservoir of puss underneath the tooth causing all the trouble, he declared that it would have to be released in order to relieve the pressure. To this end, he added an extra long "bit" to his drill and simply bored down through the tooth, the root and the nerve and out the bottom (that's the bottom of the tooth, not my bottom, although it felt like it). Thus, the gunge beneath the tooth was granted its freedom.

I'm not upsetting anyone in any way, am I? It bloody upset me, I can tell you.

Back at the cottage, there was one feature which we hadn't yet tried out. The fireplace in the main room (you could have called it a sitting room, were it not for the fact that that the only thing to sit on was a straight-backed wooden chair) was tempting. True, it did have a bird's nest in it, but it looked combustible. Besides, there being nothing else to do, we spent the evenings playing board games in the kitchen. There was a TV, but it was a black and white one with no signal. What more attractive thought than to play our board games in front of a crackling log fire?

I gathered a few twigs from the hedge, added them to the bird's nest and struck a match. Within seconds, the entire house was filled with acrid fumes and all its inhabitants were forced to flee, squelching into the yard while the - shall we say furious? - farmer poured buckets of water onto the conflagration. Well, how was I to know that the chimney had been boarded up years before?

"That's it," said Paul, "we're leaving." And, surprisingly, no one tried to talk him out of his decision.

At the height of the summer, it's not normally easy to change ferry crossings, but Paul pulled rank at P & O and arranged for us to take the next day's boat from Le Havre. But by the time we had squeezed everything back into the car, time was tight. Paul had the bit between his teeth and entered suicidal driving mode, determined on no account to miss the ferry. The rest of us just covered our eyes and prayed, while Sam expressed himself by bellowing

"Wuuuuaaaaaaaarrrgh!"

into my ear with even more urgency and frequency than before.

None of it helped. We drove onto the harbour front to witness the Pride of Le Havre (or whatever it was called) steaming purposefully out of the harbour, and not even the Queen Mother could have had it turned round. We had to book ourselves into a seedy seafront hotel for the night.

And while we're on about it, what does Le Havre have to be proud about? It's a horrible place with few redeeming features. But I may be prejudiced on account of what happened that evening when we tried to go out for a meal in what looked like quite a nice restaurant. The infant Annabel had a little plastic horse which she trotted round the table. Yes, it made a bit of noise, but the people at the only other table which was occupied showed no sign of even noticing, far less complaining. Nevertheless, the owner decided that he was going to ask us to leave, because we were "disturbing other customers". I've never been so angry. Opposite, there was a building site. I picked up a brick and had to be restrained from hurling it through the restaurant's window. I'd have done it, I honestly would.

"Let's look on the bright side," I said in the morning (another unhelpful saying, aren't they all?). "Now we've got time to do some duty-free shopping."

"Very good, Oliver. Where exactly are we going to put it?"

"Er ... on my lap?"

And so it was that I ended up with several large boxes of wine and beer on my knees in the back seat, obscuring Paul's view as he reversed out of Auchan's car park and straight into a concrete bollard which inflicted severe damage on his father-in-law's precious car.

But still we remained friends. Indeed, I'm sure that, if it hadn't been for growing children and changing relationships, we'd have shared lots more holidays. As it was, it was many years before we teamed up once more, again following one of my bright ideas.

***

In my youth, I'd avidly read the novels of Arthur Ransome. Although the most famous of them were set in the Lake District, two of my favourites, "Coot Club" and "The Big Six" had been about nineteen-twenties youngsters living out idyllic sailing holidays on the Norfolk Broads. The names resonated with me so vividly: Wroxham, Horning, Potter Heigham. What about hiring a boat on the Broads and having a few adventures ourselves? After all, both Paul and I now had two teenage children and Paul's new wife Adèle got on well with Birgit. What could go wrong?

Well, the M25, for a start. It was Friday night, and, as usual, the traffic was at a standstill in the torrential rain, but we comforted ourselves with the reassuring thought that we were heading for an area of tranquil beauty where we would be able to relax and forget the hurly-burly of daily life.

Yes, well ... Arthur Ransome was writing a long time ago. It turned out that the M25 and the Broads had more in common than one could possibly have imagined. As we took over our cruiser and pulled out onto the river, we noticed a strange similarity between what we were doing now and what we had been doing a couple of hours previously, namely making slow progress through a traffic jam. The only difference was that we were now in a boat. So there we have it: the M25 and the Norfolk Broads: Both are long, straight, featureless and permanently jammed.

Surely not? Why do so many people go on the Broads for their holidays? Ah, there's a paradox. If it wasn't for the tourists, it would be quite quiet, wouldn't it? And so would the beach at Torremolinos. Although, to be perfectly accurate, a better Broads analogy would be Tesco's car park on a Friday evening: a procession of vehicles searching fruitlessly for a parking space. This we realised when the time came for us to think about mooring for the night. Easy, we thought, remembering our canal successes. We simply tie up outside a rustic pub and dive into it for dinner.

Ah, but on the Broads, it doesn't work like that. As dusk encroached, we began to panic. Where could we tie up? Okay, theoretically, we could drop anchor in the middle of a broad, but then we wouldn't be able to go to the pub.

That was the problem, the pubs. They really have it sewn up, you know. Provided their particular piece of river bank isn't already choc-a-bloc (which it probably is), they are delighted for you to moor up outside them but only if you **a)** pay a fiver for the privilege or **b)** eat an over-priced meal in them. On the first night, we opted for the latter course, which provided us with quite an adventure.

We stumbled through the monsoon (yes, of course there was a bloody monsoon) to a large pub with a big family room. The place was packed with holidaymakers, all tucking into something or other with chips. We all commented on the fact that the chips were real (i.e. made out of actual potatoes, not frozen). How refreshing! How unusual and innovative for pub food to be genuinely home made! But not for one family in the corner, who complained to the barmaid about the quality of their chips. Far from being pleased, they would actually have preferred their chips to be of the frozen variety.

The chef was at the end of his tether after allegedly serving 300 meals that weekend. The first that we or any of the other guests knew of this was when he came charging out of the kitchen, pouring sweat and snorting and grunting like a newly-released bull. In his hand he held aloft a large raw potato, which he slammed onto the table of the complaining family with such force that he nearly broke it in two, like in one of those karate demonstrations. A hush descended on the bar as all eyes and ears turned to him.

"You wanna see a fucking potato?" he demanded. "That's a fucking potato! I don't expect you've ever seen one. In this pub you get real food. If you want frozen food, you can fuck off back to your council house where you belong!"

Obviously, political correctness is an alien concept to the good folk of Norfolk - at least to this particular representative. The balance of support seemed to be in favour of the chef, and there was even a hint of a ripple of applause, but unfortunately, he had chosen the wrong family (or the wrong family had chosen him). The father was large, tattooed and musclebound, while his wife would have given a fishwife a bad name. As the man got to his feet and drew himself up to his full and not inconsiderable height, far from restraining him and saying, "No, Gary, don't get involved", she was actually pushing him forward and encouraging him to "make something of it". It was obvious that a major brawl was about to break out, and the first thing that seemed likely to happen would be that the chef, who was overweight and not young, would collapse from a heart attack. He was as white as a sheet and hyperventilating alarmingly.

But he wasn't to be insulted in this way. As his customer squared up to him, he suddenly had an idea for a choice of weapon, charged back into the kitchen and re-emerged with a large catering container full of chips, which he proceeded to pour over the customer's head.

As the customer wiped the grease from his eyes, this was the point at which, along with the rest of the cowering clientèle, we slunk out into the car park, adults shivering and children wide-eyed. Wow, that had been some supper. It had come complete with cabaret and we hadn't even had a chance to pay, although I did go back and settle up the next morning. The bar was surprisingly un-trashed, but of the chef there was no sign.

Back on the boat, we naturally discussed the events, and it turned out that it was a good thing the chef hadn't done a Basil Fawlty and demanded to know whether the other customers were satisfied. Comparing notes about our various meals, we discovered that the salmon and prawn pie had contained neither salmon nor prawns, while the chicken curry had thrown up remarkably little chicken.

"Well, go on then, who else is dissatisfied with their meal, eh?"

You could imagine hands being timidly raised:

"Er, well, actually ...."

The pubs got better, but not much. On the second night, we were enticed to moor outside a hostelry in Horning. Here there was a man on duty especially to reel you in, like a fish. By this time, it was so wet that you could hardly tell where the river ended and the garden began, and he was appropriately attired from head to foot in bright yellow waterproofs and waders. We didn't mind that, but he then woke us up at 6 am by noisily re-arranging us in order to squeeze in yet more captive customers.

The next night we were at a pub at Reedham Ferry. By this time, we had got things better sussed and had tied up some distance away and walked into the village, at least giving us a choice of where to eat (which was a system which only worked if you could actually find a free mooring space anywhere, which was seldom). In this pub, things looked more promising until the local folk musician came on and played every cliche finger-in-the-ear folk song known to man. That bastard "Wild Rover" and "Seven Bloody Drunken Nights", you know the stuff. His set was enlivened by a girl in the audience who looked like an ex-punk rocker along the lines of Hazel O'Connor and begged to be allowed to do a song. She had a sweet voice and did a pin-dropping rendition of Ewan McColl's "The First Time Ever I Saw Her Face". Of course, she was a million times better that Mr Arran

Sweater (the Singing Postman would have been preferable) and we all bellowed for more. He was having none of it. Unwilling to have his show stolen, he tried to win us back by involving us in a lusty singalong entitled "Norfolk and Good" (try singing it out loud). The children were even wider-eyed than before, and the adults just raised their eyes to heaven.

Before finally giving in and opting for the "anchor in the middle of a broad and play board games" option, we did have one last despairing attempt at a pub supper. In Stalham, there seemed to be only one pub with food, so in we went. The ensuing scenario will be one which readers will recognise. In case any readers are foreign, you may need an introduction to the culture of pub food in the UK

Each table has a little brass plate on it with a number. Near the bar will be a poster with easy-to-follow instructions for how to get something in your stomach. On no account sit down at a table and expect to be served, because you'll be there until closing time, at which point they'll chuck you out. The instructions will say:

1. Select a table from those available and note its number.

2. Choose a dish from our delicious and wide-ranging menu and order it at the bar.

3. Order your drinks at the same time.

4. The meal will then be brought to your table *(Ed: Big deal, huh?)*.

In other words, you do all the work. Plus, by the time your food arrives, you have finished your drink. You can try asking the waitress for another one, but she will look at you as if you are from the Planet Zog and say she isn't allowed to do that. So you re-join the queue for the bar and, by the time you have obtained your drink, your food is cold.

There are, of course, some variations to this pattern, and it was one of these that we experienced in Stalham. You scan the menu and find some things which sound really nice. You order them and sit down, only to be informed some time later that they are, in fact, "off". So you have to have a re-think and return to the bar and order something you don't actually particularly want. In the meantime, those who ordered things that were "on" receive and consume theirs, leaving you all on your own with yours. Except that, in Stalham, fifty percent of the menu was "off", so at least we got to eat in two shifts.

I went for a fantastic starter. "Succulent, fresh whole-tail North Atlantic King Prawns, lightly coated in crisp golden breadcrumbs and grilled to perfection, served with a deliciously light Marie-Rose sauce and a salad garnish."

Wow! It sounded magnificent! Why do people bother going to France when they can get catering like this on their own doorstep? The reality was two reconstituted lumps of frozen fishy stuff with prawn tails attached, done up in batter and deep fried in lard until nearly black, served with a leaf of lettuce and some pink gunge from Happy Shopper.

Still, the surroundings were interesting. The very loud jukebox specialised in speed metal. We ate our second and third choices surrounded by the black leather-clad and heavily-pierced locals (whose engine oil aroma was actually preferable to that emitting from the kitchen), to the strains of Metallica, Megadeth and Slipknot. Yum!

From then on, we settled for take-away ready meals from Somerfields in Beccles.

Probably, a Broads holiday is wonderful if the sun shines, but as it was, we just had to keep on the move, which was especially problematic because the hire boat didn't have any windscreen wipers and for much of the time we couldn't see where we were going. Apart from reducing the scenic merit of the holiday, it meant we were in a permanent state of terror of crashing into the bank, a bridge or another boat.

A further problem was caused by the fact that you had to lower the entire roof before going under bridges. In the ongoing tropical storm, this was inadvisable, so various routes were inaccessible to us. At Potter Heigham, for instance, even the little dinghies favoured by Coot Club members had trouble negotiating the famously low bridge, so we had no chance at all After all the rain, there was only about a foot of clearance, so even a model boat such as you might use in your bath would have found it difficult to get through. All we could do was shrug our shoulders and turn round.

On one occasion, we rounded a corner to see a railway bridge in front of us. I don't know why no one thought to make any preparations. We just kind of assumed that it would lift itself or swing open or something. It even looked high enough for us to swish gently underneath it. As it happened, a nice little train was just passing over it, so maybe we were distracted by that. Possibly we were just pissed.

At any event, Paul suddenly yelled, "Shit, I've got to lower the roof". As I threw the engine into reverse, Paul rushed below decks to adjust the roof, but never got there. In his haste, he smashed his head against the wooden canopy, making a gaping hole in it (that's his head, not the canopy, which remained intact). The passengers in the passing train had front row seats for a splatter movie, as we drifted around in the middle of the river, lavishing the entire first aid kit upon Paul's shattered bonce.

Within two days, we had explored every available inch of the Northern Broads and were forced to take the plunge of negotiating Great Yarmouth, about which the guide book was

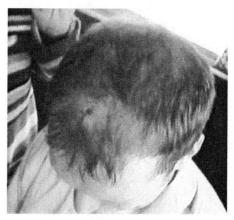

Think yourself lucky it's not in colour.

completely doom-laden, and rightly so. It was terrifying. What we had to do was consult the handbook, calculate when low tide would be at Yarmouth and set out from a place called Stracey Arms two hours beforehand, in the knowledge that the river we were travelling along was now tidal and that we would absolutely not be able to stop or moor up anywhere between there and the coast. Instructions for dealing with the various bridges, narrow channels, vicious currents, traffic lights and other hazards of Great Yarmouth were detailed and complicated. You couldn't have done it without someone reading them out loud to the steerer.

Except that some people obviously did. Here another hazard came into the equation. Not only were we incompetent landlubbers, but so was practically everyone else on the Broads. In the Arthur Ransome books, there were just one or two "Hullabaloos", or townies playing loud music, travelling too fast and generally being useless and dangerous. But here, everybody (including us) was a Hullabaloo. We had all had a laughable minimum of instruction. We, however, were at least trying to follow the rules about speed, position, etiquette, etc, while many of the others cheerfully ignored everything except their own progress, instead acting as if they were in bumper boats in a theme park. Yup, it was the old M25 syndrome again.

On the way to Great Yarmouth, therefore, we saw one terrified family stranded at 45 degrees on a mudflat, having strayed too far from the centre of the channel. It was the Broads equivalent of the hard shoulder, except with no access to any emergency telephones and a longer than usual wait for the AA.

Negotiating one of the bridges, we narrowly avoided a head-on collision with one boat while nearly being rammed from behind by another. As soon as we emerged onto Breydon Broad, a speedboat full of "Hullabaloos" streaked past, leaving the flotilla of pleasure boats bobbing and plunging and in genuine danger of sinking.

In the evenings, pubs having proved a bit of a culinary cul de sac, we took to playing games. This is the best way for families to bond, unless, of course, any of the members are particularly competitive. Luckily, no one in either family cared less whether we won or lost, so normally the evenings degenerated into stomach-ache inducing hysterics on the subject of each other's bodily functions, all of which were clearly audible through the paper-thin cabin walls. Don't go on holiday with friends if you have any intimate personal secrets you'd rather they didn't know about. And do not entertain any hopes of sex. Luckily, we all knew about each other's farting, snoring and pre-menstrual outrageousness before we set off, and we knew a hell of a lot more about them by the time we got back.

But still we remained friends. In fact, we all became even better friends, bolstered by the reassurance that each family suffered in equal measure from the wrath of female hormones and that there are certain things in life that are best let out into the open.

Paul and his family recently emigrated to America, probably in order to avoid the possibility that we might invite them on a fortnight's mountain bike tour of Milton Keynes.

Chapter 11

Carry On Camping

When we discovered camping in Ireland, I genuinely believed that we had found the solution to all our problems. What joy! Quiet, narrow, slow, almost empty roads, fantastic countryside, welcoming natives, idyllic and deserted sandy beaches and cool Guinness. This surely was the life, in every respect.

The first year was spent in the area round Galway. When we returned, brown as berries and fully rested, people thought we had been in the Caribbean. We had camped on lovely, quiet sites, lounged on deserted beaches, been for midnight swims, cooked evening meals on the beach, visited scarcely inhabited islands, indulged in extravagant seafood suppers, and drunk the entire European Guinness Lake. We had come to terms with the two essentials of dining out in Ireland, which are that lemonade is red and that plain crisps are actually cheese and onion. And so we vowed to return.

The plan was to attack the Ring of Kerry, praised by all as the most scenically beautiful part of Ireland. I looked at a map and found a place called Waterville which looked as if it was nearby. Probably I got confused with Waterford, famous for its crystal glass factory, I don't know. Did I dream it or hadn't I once read that Tiger Woods liked to limber up for European matches by playing a round or two at Waterville? It seemed likely that it would be a lovely place, and there was a campsite there.

Have you ever put up a tent in the rain? It's a dispiriting activity, because, no matter how careful you are, all your bedding is going to be sodden before you even climb into it for the first time. Plus, we had the heaviest and most complicated tent ever manufactured. Never mind, we thought, it's bound to be all right in the morning.

It wasn't, of course. We had pitched our tent where they told us to, which was at the bottom of a valley. By the morning, the accumulated moisture from the torrential storm which had gone on all night had come together to form a small lake underneath us. But we weren't actually waterlogged, because, with a built-in groundsheet, we were regally floating on the surface. The effect was akin to sleeping in a water bed, and initially not unpleasant. It certainly was particularly pleasurable for the ardent young Dutch couple camped in a tiny tent immediately adjacent to us. They had discovered a way both of keeping warm and of utilising the water bed, which explained the rhythmic squelching noises which had been emitting from it all night. Most offputting.

The children spent the next couple of days cooped up in the site's tiny "Kids' Room" which showed, through a soup of condensation, a never-ending sequence of flickering Tom and Jerry videos. They consumed cheese and onion crisps ("But I asked for plain crisps." - "These **are** plain crisps.") and drank lemonade ("But why's it red?" - Because it's made from lemons." "Oh ...").

Well, we were in Ireland.

Birgit and I put on a brave face and lay in the tent all day, saying things like, "It's nice to be able to catch up on some reading, isn't it?" (*Thinks: Is it bollocks*). Occasionally, we donned our wellies and went for a few half-hearted walks under the umbrella. Surely Tiger Woods could find somewhere more exciting than this? It was very depressing.

In the evenings, we walked into Waterville to try and find something to eat. Waterville, it seemed, was the only place in the entire Republic of Ireland without the slightest hint of any "*Craic*". The two pubs were both peopled entirely with red-faced, leering alcoholics. Outside on the seafront, there was one of those tiny travelling funfairs run by tattooed young psychopaths. Each year, there are news headlines when some unfortunate youngster plunges to his or her death from some "ride" or other at one of these fairs. The children begged to be allowed to participate, so we gave them some money, looked the other way and trembled. Everything was utterly dismal.

We called the campsite owner "Mr Grump". Anything was too much trouble for him. He spent the whole time being beastly to polite foreigners, threatening to beat up his children and taking pleasure in answering "No" to every question he was asked. We had to escape.

Ireland is famous for its Bed and Breakfasts, so off we set to Dingle and booked into a representative B & B., which was just as you'd expect a B & B to be. (Cor, that's alliteration, I think.) The pink sheets were made of Lycra and stuck to us. We felt as if we were intruding into someone else's private territory (which we effectively were) and had to get up early for a gigantic, greasy Irish Breakfast (that's an English Breakfast, served in Ireland).

If you've had loads of Guinness the night before (and if you're in Ireland and haven't drunk loads of Guinness, there's something wrong with you), not only will your morning movement be pitch black, but your stomach will be so bloated that you can manage, at most, one cornflake, half a mushroom and one bite of toast. The breakfast is completely wasted, but you unfortunately don't have the option to ask for just B without the B.

The problem we had was that the B & B very rapidly consumed all our money. We had to have two rooms, and at £25 a head, that meant that we were paying, for the four of us, hang on a minute, oh yes, £100. Well, you can't keep that up for long, can you? We lasted two days, during which the weather meant that we had to stay permanently in the rooms, lying desolately on the beds. All the books we had brought with us were rapidly read and then swapped, with the result that I ended up reading the latest epic by Maeve Binchey, while Birgit struggled valiantly with a biography of the Sex Pistols.

We checked out Fungi, Dingle's pet dolphin (and yes, the family were all seasick) and suffered even more financial hardship as a result of the town's not really deserved reputation as a gourmet centre. In fact, in Dingle, I paid the most I have ever paid in my entire life for a meal. I kept the bill in my scrapbook and still come over faint every time I see it. Was the meal any good? I can't remember.

There was nothing for it but to go home early. To admit defeat in this way felt humiliating, but we had close on run out of money, and sitting round indoors getting on each other's nerves was surely something one could do better and more economically at home. Admittedly, even with a widget, canned Guinness is nothing like the real thing, but perhaps that was a sacrifice worth making. So we rang up, changed the ferry booking and set off back towards Rosslare.

"Hang on, did you see that?"

"What?"

"That house had a 'To Let' sign in the window."

Screeech.

This was half way round the Dingle peninsula. It was a fairly dilapidated-looking little whitewashed bungalow, but it offered shelter. The owner explained that she had been let down at the last minute and that we could have it for the entire week for £100. We were saved.

"Hello? Is that the ferry company? We want to cancel the new booking and revert to the old one."

"Pardon?"

Okay, well, it did continue to rain without pause the entire time we were there, but at least the cottage was ours, we were dry and we weren't stowing away in someone else's boat (metaphorically speaking, ha, ha). We played lots and lots of cards, bought a few more books, and lived on Heinz Spaghetti in Tomato Sauce.

One especially wonderful thing about Ireland, we discovered, is the Rose of Tralee competition. We knew to our cost that we were near Tralee, having spent an afternoon in one of those nightmarish swimming pool complexes where you catch verucas and get kicked in the face by horrible young children who emerge at high velocity from a flume, smack you in the gob and splash chlorine-filled water into your eyes, so that you wake up the next morning thinking you've gone blind because your eyelids are gummed together and you can't open them.

The Rose of Tralee is a televised beauty competition of refreshing civilisation. The girls aren't bathing beauties at all, but appear in full evening dress, having travelled from all over the world. Thus, you get Maraig O'Donnell, the Icelandic Rose, Maeve O'Brien, the Liechtenstein Rose, and Sinead O'Shaughnessy, the Outer Mongolian Rose. Of course, they are interviewed by Gay Byrne, because Gay Byrne is Ireland's only TV presenter. There are no others.

The girls are all so demure and, well, rose-like, that it holds a fascination unlike any other beauty competition. It certainly doesn't feel in any way politically incorrect to watch it. Mind you, we did have to turn up the volume a lot. The wind was howling round the cottage in a terrifying way, and, as we watched, dear old Gay was doing his best to retain his composure. The storm was so violent, he explained, that the marquee in which the event was to have been staged had completely blown away. As he spoke, a huge cast of extras behind him was physically lugging the stage set into the town hall, where the emergency relocation was taking place.

The Roses were all completely unfazed as they dealt with Gay's interrogation. The Australian Rose, for example, was a plain-clothes police officer whose ambition was to become the next female Police Commissioner, and her greatest desire was to meet Mary Robinson and George Clooney, presumably not together. The Californian Rose was studying medicine at UCLA and her hobbies were opera and hiking. No bimbos, these Roses, as the pot plants swayed and toppled behind them. We all voted for the wrong ones, but what the heck.

It was a half-mile walk into the nearest village, a place called Ballyferriter which must, surely, have featured in some Ballykissangel-style twee Irish TV show or film, so perfect was it. All the buildings were painted in different pastel colours and virtually all of them were pubs. There were rows and rows of them. We naturally used the weather as an excuse to spend every single evening in them, playing cards with complete strangers and generally revelling in the *Craic*, which was here much in evidence. On any night of the week, this tiny village offered a choice of five or six different styles of live music. You don't find that everywhere, do you?

Down at the end of the Dingle peninsula was an astonishing place. The Blasket island centre is a concrete monstrosity which couldn't be more out of place, rearing up incongruously out of the wild landscape. I came over all Prince Charles-ish, pronounced it a carbuncle and refused to enter it.

This was a grave error. I declared that it would be a much better idea to visit the prehistoric stone "beehive huts" which clustered in fields at the apex of the peninsula, but unfortunately, the rain was so torrential that we ended up trapped in one for over an hour. Considering that people had seemingly been pissing and crapping in them for centuries, the experience was less than pleasant and I was in terrible trouble with the family.

The Blasket Island Centre, once we ("Oh, all right then, if I have to") got inside it, was warm, comfortable and totally fascinating. Audio-visual displays told the intriguing story of the islands and their way of life as the numbers of inhabitants dwindled. Their stories were uniquely moving, and the museum was set out in such a personal, un-stuffy way that you really felt you got to know these brave people. Obviously, a trip out to the islands was going to be necessary.

The Great Blasket must be one of the most intriguing places on earth. The island retains a complete ghost village. Although no one has lived there since 1953, the buildings remain intact, just as if they were inhabited. The desolate beauty of the landscape lends it an almost spiritual feel. This means that, if you buy one of the books about life on the island, such as *The Islandman*, you can picture exactly how it must have been.

As it turned out, we had concerns which were closer to home. We had walked to the far end of the island when we heard the horn of the ferry hooting urgently in the distance. The skipper had warned us that a storm might be in the offing, and that we should return to the boat immediately if he gave the signal. As a bean soup fog overwhelmed us (that's a pea soup fog, only thicker), we stumbled through the heather, made the ferry just as it was about to cast off, abandoning any remaining passengers, and made the short crossing back to the mainland with moments to spare before the storm struck. If we hadn't got there in time, said the skipper, we might have had to shelter for days in one of the abandoned cottages.

As everyone but me puked their way back to England on the so-called Sea-Cat to Fishguard (cats do puke a lot, it's true, but surely that's not how those fast but stomach-heaving vessels got their name), we reflected that, completely broke and sniffling as we were, we could no longer safely embark on any more camping holidays in Ireland. The tent took three days on the lawn before it was dry enough to be packed away ready for another day.

**

"What do you mean, another day?" said Birgit and the girls. "There isn't going to be another day. We don't care what you say, next year we are going somewhere hot and dry."

"Yes, yes, all right. But we can still use the tent, can't we? The South of France is probably quite nice, and we can camp there without any fear of hypothermia."

"Well, if you say so ..."

Before that, we actually had to get to the South of France. Travelling long distances is a major problem for our family, because I suffer from a motorway phobia (not such an uncommon thing as you might imagine), which means that Birgit has to do all the driving. The girls both hate being cooped up, both get travel sick and both complain about how hot, uncomfortable and generally unbearable the journey is.

"Open the window."

"No, close it."

"But I'm too hot."

"And I'm in a draught."

"Turn the radio on."

"No, not that station."

"I can't hear it."

"That's because you've got the window open."

"Well then, close it."

"But then it'll be too hot."

"Let's play a game."

"All right, what?"

"Twenty questions."

"No, I don't like that."

"When are we there?"

Seconds after arriving in France, we were charging down the *autoroute*. Motorway phobia? What motorway phobia? I found myself saying to the family, "You know, maybe motorways aren't so bad after all". It was Sunday lunchtime and the *autoroute* was almost picturesque, its central reservation crammed with attractive flowering shrubs, and there was not a single car, lorry, caravan or "*mobil-home*" in sight. I was cured!

Twenty-four hours later, we were reaching for the Valium again. South of Dijon, the lorries were back, the Dutch and the Germans had arrived, the Brits had caught up and the *péage* was once again the Highway To Hell. In fact, it was just Hell, full stop.

Now we realised why we'd been warned never to drive the length of France. What was worse, we'd just worked out that, by the time we added up all the petrol and the frequent and astronomical *péage* tolls, it would have been almost as cheap to put the car on the train and travel without terror.

People love national stereotyping when it comes to drivers, but it really doesn't matter where they come from, as soon as they hit the French *péage*, they all go completely crazy. It's almost as if they're saying, look, we've paid for this, so we'll do what we like. "What we like" consisted in this case of switching lanes without indicating, weaving in and out of traffic like a snake, exceeding the speed limit as a matter of honour, flashing, hooting and gesticulating and, above all, seeing how close they could get to the car in front while travelling at a hundred miles an hour.

The *autoroute* had magnificent signing. One of the most useful notices was a frequent and gigantic hoarding pointing out in pictorial fashion that you needed to keep at least two of the white lines they had helpfully painted at the side of the road between you and the next car. If not, it said, you would certainly be dead should the car in front choose to brake suddenly.

Fine. Great stuff. Except that not a single person took any notice of it whatsoever. The authorities might as well have saved themselves the millions of francs the warning signs undoubtedly cost. I decided that it was just human beings exercising their right to take risks, like they do by smoking, mountaineering and walking backwards to the North Pole in their pyjamas. The only trouble was that they were taking risks with the lives of me and my family as well as their own.

So it wasn't surprising that every few kilometres, there was a pile-up. We saw a Dutch caravan which had ended up vertical rather than horizontal, numerous shunts and one scene where people were being laid out by the side of the road. The thing to look out for was a sudden blaze of brake lights and hazard warning lights immediately in front of you. This was a signal for Birgit to slam on the brakes and do likewise, hoping that the person behind would be reasonably alert.

The *péage* had huge and very impressive gantries which provided you with useful information such as "belt up in the back" (observed as much as the "keep your distance" signs were) or advance notice that the next *"aire"* would provide live entertainment for children. But the big one to watch out for was *"Bouchon"*. This, conveniently, is a direct translation of the English word "Bottleneck", and what it meant was, keep going at the same outrageous speed, but be ready to leap on your brakes and switch on your flashers at any moment.

As we struggled though Provence, something really peculiar happened. One of the many ignored signs is one advising drivers to "take a break". This is something you can actually do in France (as opposed to in the UK) because every few kilometres there are very nice little *"aires"*, or resting places.

Being obedient, we decided to do just that, and the three attractive females in the family promptly lay down on a blanket and fell asleep. I, the unattractive male member of the family, went to the loo and was startled, on my return, to find that a battered old Renault had parked next to the girls. In it were two young Marti Pellow clones (dark, pony-tailed, handsome, unshaven), who were observing the girls closely.

Having just read a newspaper article about motorway bandits, I momentarily and mistakenly sensed trouble, until it became clear that they had merely broken down. The Renault wouldn't start, so I offered them a push. It did the trick, the engine spluttered into life (yes it did, it spluttered) and they set off down the slip road. But then, inexplicably, they started to reverse, and came all the way back to us.

"What's the problem?" I asked.

"We want to say *merci*," replied Marti One.

"Oh, that's okay."

Marti Two cupped his hand to his mouth and inhaled, imitating taking a drag on a joint.

"Would you like to '*fume*' something?"

Aha! So it wasn't only hairstyles they had in common with Marti Pellow. I declined the offer.

"Une bière, peut-être?"

"No thanks, we're driving."

So, with friendly waves and cries of *"Bonne route"*, we parted company and they drove off.

"Do you think we'll ever see them again?" wondered the girls, secretly smitten.

We would. At the next *péage* toll barrier, the Two Martis had been pulled over and their car was being disembowelled by several *gendarmes*. I felt awful, simultaneously guilty and not guilty. After all, if I hadn't done them the good turn of giving them a push, they wouldn't have been busted.

There must be a moral here. It's just that I can't work out what it is.

***

One thing I knew for sure was that I wouldn't be going near any of those "Instant Camping For Inadequate Brits" French campsites. Come on, they are to actual camping what fast food is to actual food. Why don't they just call themselves McCamp or Kentucky Fried Camping and have done with it?

I mean, those tents. They're all identical and laid out in rows, like goods on a supermarket shelf. If you came home pissed late at night, you'd probably end up in bed with your neighbour's wife.

And then just look inside them. That's not a tent, it's a branch of IKEA. It's got things like beds, fridges and cupboards that no genuine camper could possibly have any use for.

"Tish," I said, "it's a disgrace."

"Hmm," said the rest of my family, "that looks nice. Why haven't we got any facilities like that?"

"Because we haven't paid through the nose for them, for a start. Have you seen the prices they pay for those places? I wouldn't expect to pay that for a week in the Ritz."

But unfortunately, when we got to the South of France, my insistence that we would certainly find a rustic campsite completely free from any British holidaymakers, and preferably free of any human beings at all, other than us, proved more than misplaced. Every campsite was chock full and most of them were of the "Could just as well be in Skegness, apart from the fact that the sun is shining" variety. Having failed to find any kind of alternative, we humiliatingly had to arrange to pitch our tent in the small corner of the Skegness Special set aside for those who were so backward as to travel with their own camping gear (which I had mistakenly thought was actually the point of camping).

These campsites are advertised as if they actually were the Ritz. The brochure for this one emphasised its proximity to the sea, its swimming pool and tennis courts, its entertainment for children and its *calme et confort*.

What it didn't mention was that it was in England. Well, not physically, you understand, but in every other way it was effectively in England, because virtually all the other campers there were English. Nothing wrong with that (I suppose), it's just that if I had wanted to spend my holidays with my fellow nationals, I'd have gone to Cornwall.

As it was, even the *Guide Michelin* for the region listed the facilities of the site and it sounded wonderful. But, oddly enough, the guide did not mention that the entire place had been taken over by those "Kentucky Fried Camping" organisations. "All you do is drive here and we'll do the rest", is their message.

How do they get away with it? Easy. It is because of the good old British fear of having to communicate in a foreign language. Even if you are worried about your ability to write a letter booking a camping space, any British campsite guide for France contains pro-forma letters of application in French, where all you need to do is fill in your name and address and the date. But even this is too intimidating. Far better to get someone else to do all the work.

It's terribly upsetting. The children of half these campers are getting 'A' Grades in their French GCSEs, for goodness sake. If they can't write a letter of reservation to a campsite, what can they do? Absolutely nothing, is the sad answer. Just watch and listen to them. The environment in which they find themselves leads them to believe they are still in England. In horror and amazement, I made notes about what I overheard people saying. This is in deepest France, remember:

"Morning mate! Loaf of bread please."

"Portion of chips please!"

"When's the swimming pool open?"

"Half of lager, please."

Loaf of bread! Half of lager! Oh God, it's depressing.

With a phrase book and the teeniest-weeniest bit of effort, they could have made any of the above requests in French with ease, but no, they were too stupid, too lazy, too arrogant, too inadequate ... whatever it was, they just couldn't be bothered. They were not prepared to attempt a single sentence in French.

Instead, they favoured playing rounders and cricket with their English friends, and didn't go outside the campsite for a single meal because they were worried about ordering.

The people running the site were, of course, turning all this to their own advantage. Putting the menu at the site restaurant and take-away in (sort of) English ensured that the campers would eat there at inflated prices rather than cheaper and better 100 yards down the road. The cooks cheerfully served all-comers in super English:

"Plateau of seafruits? Certainly, sir."

I observed one English lady who was on no account going to let the word *"croissant"* pass her lips:

"One of those, please," she said, pointing at it suspiciously.

Sometimes it was extremely hard to get vital messages across to the campers. The proprietors seemed very intent on making sure that nobody entered the swimming pool wearing standard shorts. Well, they had a point. It would be tempting to spend the whole day sweating into these and then gain refreshment by leaping straight into the pool, but the hygiene of such an action would be questionable.

Fifty yards from the pool, there was a poster: *"Short interdit!"*, it read. A bit later on, another sign proclaimed, in English, "Swimming briefs only." As you entered the pool area, another sign wearily told you, "These are swimming briefs," pointing to a pair of trunks displayed on a hanger.

I did have an altercation with the bronzed young student who acted as pool supervisor. There was a rule that you had to walk through a small basin of water before entering the pool. By the end of the afternoon, this lukewarm puddle was full of fag ends and bits of fluff from between people's toes, but he spotted me walking round it rather than through it and told me off. Now one adult ticking off another adult in public (especially a teacher, who is used to being the teller-offer) is embarrassing, so I pointed out that it would actually have been less hygienic to have walked through the basin than round it. This comment was made, for a change, in a loud voice and in English, thus ensuring that several other bathers joined in on my side. We didn't win the argument, but at least he got a little net and fished out the fag ends.

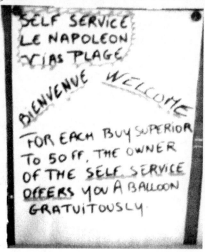

The things they do in France: Gratuitous Balloon Offering.

The rather clever secret weapon employed by the owners was not to supply information in English if they didn't really want the Brits around on any given occasion. Thus, the advertisements for the *"Tournoi de boules"* and the *"Tournoi de ping-pong"* were pointedly written in French only. Sure enough, it worked like a charm and not a single British camper registered for either.

Well, with the greatest of respect to my countrymen, I didn't want to spend any time in France fraternising with English people. Just observing their activities was shocking. Most of them had brought corn flakes, baked beans and Marmite (okay, we'll forgive them that one) with them, and every day, they packed their children off into the custody of red-uniformed young students who occupied them with games which seemed to have rather suspect military undertones, involving marching round the site chanting football slogans. In the evenings, there were entertainments such as, oh God, karaoke and quiz sessions. Here, the owners once again triumphed by including questions about politics and geography which none of the British campers could answer. As a result, the quizzes, despite being set in English, were always won by someone from France, Scandinavia or Holland.

The mornings were the worst time at Tent-U-Like. The nights were pretty shit as well. Just yards away from our tent was a pulsating disco which only opened up a couple of hours after we had gone to bed. It was like a gigantic version of one of those annoying cars which make booming noises while waiting at traffic lights. I'm sure that, if you could have seen the building in the dark, it would have been pumping like those hearts you see on gruesome TV documentaries about cardiac surgery. From inside, you could just make out the DJ wittering between the records:

"Wurrawarrrhawhehawhehoollie ..."

"Quoi? Taisez-vous!" No chance.

At about 5 am, this would eventually die down, only to be replaced by the twittering, bleeping, squawking dawn chorus set up by the inhabitants of the many trees of the wood in which the campsite was situated. I can tell you that, despite being a paid-up member of the League Against Cruel Sports, I'd have shot every last one of the bastards, had a suitable firearm been available.

Another prime target for assassination was the effusively enthusiastic *"animateur"* at the swimming pool, who was also an early riser. Shortly after the birds had completed their welcome to the day and gone off for a fly somewhere, his booming voice would come blasting over the P.A., accompanied by a piercing screech of feedback:

"Geeeeeuuuuurd meuuurrneeeeeng, lurseeeez ernd sheurntlemeurn. Aurt zee sweurmeeng pearl, zaire ease a seursssieurn euve Aaaaakwa-Sheeeeeeeeeem!!!!!!!!"

Well, bugger me if half the campers didn't just think this was a fabulous idea, and rush off to join in the *Aaaaakwa-Sheeeeeeeeeem*, which was itself, of course, accompanied by a deafening sequence of hugely amplified instructions.

So, as any form of natural sleep was impossible, we had to create a virtual reality set of sleep-friendly circumstances. This we did with the aid of some equipment thoughtfully provided by some friends who had travelled somewhere by Virgin Atlantic: free socks, earplugs and eye-masks. When I retire, I'm going to invent a tent which has double glazing and sound insulation. It'll make me rich.

Throughout our sojourn at Butlins-Sur-Mer, I insisted on pretending not to be English. This could occasionally be a double-edged sword. We bought a set of *boules*, which immediately meant that all the Brits assumed we were French. It was fun to cause traffic gridlock by playing on the gravel roads running through the campsite. On one occasion, as we were purposely clogging up the exit, some joker called out,

"Get out of the way, Froggies."

"We're not Froggies, actually."

"Oh, sorry, we just thought ..."

"Yeah, well, you thought wrong."

The next day, a tiny French boy insisted that we had stolen his *cochonet* (the little wooden ball that you throw your boules at). When we assured him that it was ours, he declared, "*Je vais chercher Papa.*"

This was a bit frightening, and became even more so when Papa turned out to be a large person with a shaved head, tattoos and earrings, not at all French-looking. However, a major international incident was avoided when Papa immediately spotted his son's *cochonet* lying under a bush, gave him a clip round the rear and invited us back to his tent for a beer.

Another French family, impressed (I hope) by our unusual willingness to act as if we were in France, insisted that we should join them one evening as they barbecued some fish they had caught. We couldn't think quickly enough of a polite way of refusing, and so ended up chewing our way through some unidentified *poisson* which had the substance of leather, the bones of a dinosaur and the taste of soiled underpants. We were all heartily sick.

Eating out in France is vital, of course. We had some French friends staying nearby, who asked us to join them in their favourite restaurant, the best in the area, they assured us. They had been going there for years. We drove miles into the country to an establishment whose speciality was food grilled "*au feu de bois*", i.e. over a wood fire. There, we experienced an evening which would have put Fawlty Towers to shame.

A sign declared that the restaurant was under new management. The waiter took our order and disappeared into the kitchen. As I passed by on the way to the loo, I saw that he was taking off his black waiter's jacket and replacing it with a white cook's one. There was no other member of staff. On the way back, I watched with fascination as he tried and failed, amid much muttering and cursing, to set light to a small pile of twigs. Eventually, he poured some lighter fluid onto it, causing a temporary conflagration which threatened to set him alight as well as the twigs.

Over our aperitifs, we watched, horrified, as black smoke belched from the kitchen, threatening to asphyxiate us all. After an hour and a half, we tentatively enquired as to when our supper might be expected to arrive. The waiter/chef's reply became, over the years, a helpful by-word, suitable for use in any fraught circumstances:

"*Soyez cool, merde!*" (Be cool, shit!)

We declined to remain cool and went off for a pizza in town.

Towards the end of our stay, a small black and white poster appeared on a tree at the entrance to the campsite. It seemed to be advertising a magic show. Where was this to take place? Underneath the glossy photo of a mysterious-looking young couple with some doves, lay the answer: "*Derrière les sanitaires*". What? Not on the main stage by the bar? No, that was for more important things, such as karaoke.

One could only assume that the career of *Erlina et Bernard* (for it was they) was no longer at its peak, if the optimal venue they could find was "behind the bogs". And behind the bogs it was, attended only by a small handful of French campers (plus us, of course), because no one else had been able to understand the poster.

It was very much a case of "Hi-de-Hi", as poor *Erlina et Bernard*, looking considerably older than on the poster, gave a stunning performance, including some very convincing levitation and some genuine doves, one of which upsettingly flew off into the toilet. The audience consisted of a few grubby and inattentive young children, who kept saying things like "You had it up your sleeve" and "It's a double-sided card". The worst indignity was the constant stream of Limey campers pushing past them to get to the loo ("'Scuse me, mate"), and the frequent farting and flushing noises emitting from within.

Of course, I couldn't allow *Erlina et Bernard* to take that away as their lasting impression of that evening's performance, so, after the show, I engaged them in conversation. They showed me their press clippings, demonstrating that they had, in better days, headlined at prestigious Paris theatres. By the time we parted, they had convinced themselves (quite without any justification) that I was single-handedly going to resurrect their career by booking them on a major tour of UK theatres. When we got home, a huge parcel of *Erlina et Bernard* posters and flyers was waiting on the doorstep.

Erlina et Bernard: They could have been big.

There are a number of depressing aspects of spending summer holidays in France. The first is the gigantic "Back To School!" posters which greet you as soon as you arrive. Because the French schoolchildren's term often starts earlier than ours, all the hypermarkets are eager to get their parents to spend their money, not on uniforms, since they very sensibly don't have any, but on pens, rulers, exercise books, etc. So, just as you think that you can forget about school for a few weeks, the first thing you see as you disembark is a massive hoarding reminding you of the *"Rentrée"*. It's cruel.

But after a couple of relaxing weeks, you eventually have to return home. This applied to us as well, although whether "relaxing" was an appropriate word was debatable. The return ferry journey was unspeakably dismal.

You'd think that, what with their astronomical prices, they'd try to make a ferry crossing a bit more sophisticated, but do they heck. What with the "resident duo" droning out a computerised version of "Tie A Yellow Ribbon", the seedy "casino" where some Phillipino girls were fleecing gullible lorry drivers, and the exorbitant self-service restaurant, we felt inclined just to stay on the boat and return to France.

It's the stark contrast to your French experience which adds to the come-down, unless, of course, you've never left Tent-U-Like. My stomach churned with depression as I saw the fare on offer: Lasagne, Battered Cod or Chilli Con Carne, all of them mass-produced and rapidly congealing under one of those things like a sun ray lamp. Welcome back to reality, it seemed to say.

"That'll be four pounds fifty, then," said the sleepy girl at the checkout.

"When?" I asked, in what I thought was a jovial manner.

"Now," she replied, uncomprehendingly.

"It was just that you said ... oh, never mind."

I had put some tea on my tray. How had we survived for a fortnight without English tea, served in its inimitable fashion? Yes, we can communicate across the world in milliseconds, we can fly to the moon, but can we invent a teapot that doesn't dribble down your wrist, scald you and drip onto your trousers, making it look as if you've wet yourself? Apparently not.

But, welcome home, because here on the ferry, the tea came in one of those uniquely English little stainless steel pots with the splatter-gun effect. One of the many disadvantages of these pots is the fact that they contain just over one cup of tea. When you want to replenish your cup, the teabag has made the remaining drop of tea undrinkably strong.

Like many people, I am in the habit of asking for some additional hot water when I pay for the tea, to avoid having to return to the queue afterwards. It's normally not a problem at all, but to this particular checkout girl, unimpressed by my previous ribaldry, it was incomprehensible.

"Could I have some extra hot water, please?" I requested, cheerfully.

She looked at me and hesitated. Then, with unerring logic, she gave her response:

"I think you'll find it's quite hot enough as it is."

Yes, we were on our way home. Maybe it was time to seek out some other forms of Conventional Family Holiday.

Chapter 12

I Am Normal

There came a time when the children started to notice that their friends were having Conventional Family Holidays and they weren't. As their classmates returned bronzed from the Canary Islands telling exciting tales of discos, theme parks and "banana rides" (not sure what these are but I'm sure I'd disapprove), the children began demanding to know why all they got offered were freezing Irish campsites and cramped canal boats.

But this was a major problem, because my experience in Majorca had truly scarred me for life. It had developed into what was virtually a phobia of package holidays (there's probably a medical term for the condition), so anything out of a glossy brochure was out of the question.

Suddenly, someone came up with the idea of ski-ing. This seemed an ideal solution, as it was a Conventional Family Holiday that we all liked the idea of. But still I had to be awkward. There was no way I was going to go to Luton and get on a plane full of jolly Brits heading for a concrete hotel somewhere in the French Alps, determined to exploit the *après-ski* to the full. No, any ski-ing holiday of ours would have to be completely independent.

Some of Birgit's relatives recommended a village in Austria called Ramsau am Dachstein. We devised a method of getting there which involved flying to Munich and then taking a series of trains. From the station in Schladming, a minibus picked us up and snaked its way up to Ramsau. This was really exciting, because as we got higher and higher, the pine trees became more and more laden with snow. It seemed just like the real thing (probably because it was).

The little flat we had booked turned out to be a stone's throw both from the ski-lifts and the village square, complete with a picture postcard church and twinkling lights. Of concrete hotels and rowdy holidaymakers there was not the slightest hint; all you could hear was the tinkling of cowbells. We were on to a winner!

The next morning provided a shock. We booked the entire family into a ski school and hired the requisite gear. Blimey! The cost was considerably more than we had budgeted for the entire week, and we hadn't even gone to the supermarket yet. I took a deep breath and wrote out a Eurocheque for gigantic lumps of plastic to put on our feet and some outfits which bore a suspicious resemblance to shell suits.

Ramsau, which at the time was in the throes of making an ultimately unsuccessful bid to host the Winter Olympics, is famous for its many miles of prepared routes for *"Langlauf"*, which is cross-country ski-ing. As this seemed a relatively un-dangerous occupation, Birgit and I decided to opt for it.

The poor children, meanwhile, were booked for the entire week onto an all-day downhill ski-ing course, which they hated. It entailed having a daily lunch consisting of things they wouldn't eat, and struggling with the instructor's strong Austrian accent.

I'd imagined cross-country ski-ing to be nice and flat, but it turned out to involve quite a lot of fairly steep hills. The movement you have to make is quite awkward, a sort of trotting motion, made more difficult by the fact that the skis are only tenuously attached to your feet. While everyone else, including Birgit, swished off confidently (even though it was a beginners' group), I ended up in a tangled heap on the ground. What was worse, the ebullient instructor kept shouting orders at me. It was probably quite good-natured, but one teacher does not take kindly to being told off by another.

"Piss off," I would mutter, not quite under my breath.

"Ha, ha. Piss off, piss off!"

I think he thought the expression had something to do with the word "Piste", meaning ski-track. One hopes he didn't address any other English-speaking guests in that manner.

The secret of my uselessness soon came out. While I was a complete beginner, the other students were only beginners at *Langlauf*. They had all had prior experience of downhill ski-ing, and therefore of the vital *"Schneepflug"* ("snow plough"") action, which is what you use to slow yourself down and generally keep in control. When we reached the first downhill bit, through some woods, everyone else just plunged down it. Being last (of course), I wasn't going to do that. I stood on the brink and quivered.

"Come on, Oliver. Best foot forward!" shouted the instructor.

"But how am I going to stop?"

"*Schneepflug, Schneepflug!*"

"*Bitte?*"

Not only was I not versed in the technique, I had never heard of it. But everyone else had disappeared and wouldn't take kindly to their lunch in a rustic ski-lodge being held up by the actions (or inactions) of a coward, so I took a deep breath and pushed myself off the edge.

A prepared *Langlauf* track consists of two quite deep grooves in the snow, and I kind of assumed that they would work like a railway track and keep me on the right lines. This was not the case. After a few metres, the track veered round to the right, but I didn't. I plunged into the forest, coming to rest splattered against a tree.

For some reason, Hans seemed to think this was hilarious. He pointed and shook with laughter.

"Piss off."

"Ja, ja, piss off, piss off."

I didn't really want to give up half way through my first day. because everything else was lovely: the sunshine, the clean air, the impeccable freshness of the scene. Also, I could go along in a straight line reasonable efficiently, so I reached a compromise whereby, whenever we came to a hill, I simply unstrapped the skis, put them over my shoulder and walked down the side of the track. Everyone else went on ahead, with the result that I had my lunch half an hour later than them, but otherwise the schedule was unaffected.

At the end of the week, there were some races. Birgit did quite well, I came last and so did the children. They had sort of enjoyed learning the basics in ski school and were given some kind of consolation prize. So, all in all, the Conventional Family Holiday had been such a success that we resolved to save up and come back the following year.

It was obvious that I was going to have to learn that damn *Schneepflug*, so this time it was decided that we would all do downhill ski-ing. But as we zig-zagged up through the woods from the station, something was different. A different colour, in fact, green, to be precise. There was no snow.

No problem, we were assured. All that would happen would be that a bus would take us further up the mountain to where there actually was some snow. So off we went to the hire shop, where the gear was even more breathtakingly expensive than the previous year - although at least this time I was mentally prepared. We were all (including the girls, rather to their chagrin) put into beginners' groups.

There, for me, the trouble began. My teacher was a precocious fifteen-year-old girl called Petra, who made it crystal clear that all her students, particularly me, were beneath her contempt. Straining at the leash, she wanted nothing other than to be charging down some mountainside at suicidal speed (a skill which she jealous-makingly demonstrated at every opportunity) rather than teaching dunces how to do the *Schneepflug*.

One of my many failings in life is an almost complete lack of any kind of ambition. After the first day, I had more or less mastered the *Schneepflug*, which meant that I could go up the almost horizontal nursery slope on a nice slow lift, and gently coast down it again. That was all I wanted to do, but Petra had other plans. In order to fulfil her desire to hurl herself down sheer slopes, she had to take us up into more dangerous territory. The next day, she announced, we would all be heading further up the mountain, where we would learn new skills.

For me, there was no next day. In the evening, we attended the weekly welcoming ski display. This was an admittedly impressive but also annoying event starring bronzed, handsome, hunky ski instructors demonstrating their skills at turning somersaults and leaping through flaming hoops. Worse, tiny infants hardly taller than garden gnomes would thunder down precipices as casually as you or I would stroll down the garden path. How on earth did they do it? Had they no fear at all? The answer was no, they didn't.

And then there were those damn snowboarders. These were testosterone-filled teenagers taking part in an activity whose sole purpose was to show off how bloody clever they were. And they were clever, and everyone, quite rightly, was in awe of them. I hated them, the bastards. But at least it seemed to be a productive way of channelling their energy. In Britain, they merely get drunk and beat the shit out of each other.

On the way home, the lack of snow meant that we were walking on sheet ice, but, following a couple of *Glühweins*, I stepped out confidently in my unsuitable footwear. In a graceful arc worthy of the best ice dancer, I found myself flying through the air before landing flat on my back. I was completely winded, but aware that I had landed on something soft. Oh my God, it was Lucy. A brief investigation revealed that she was nothing more than shocked, but I was in severe pain. I had cracked a rib, an agonising injury that meant that any further ski-ing was out of the question.

In a way, it was a lucky escape, because I know I'd have hated to be up the mountain with the ghastly Petra. But I had, in fact, already decided to quit the class and spend the whole week swishing up and down the nursery slope. This I found delightfully relaxing and absolutely sufficient from a stimulation point of view. But it was not to be. I spent the entire week immobile, watching daytime quiz shows on Austrian TV. Birgit, meanwhile, discovered the way to become a brave and skilled downhill ski-er. Her group went up to a ski-lodge and became involved in a game which entailed drinking enormous amounts of schnapps. They then blasted down the mountain through the woods, pissed out of their brains and without a care in the world.

In the end-of-the-week competition, the girls came last. Again. So, of course, we didn't go back to Ramsau. Oh yes we did. Feeling cheated of my full entitlement the previous year, I agreed to give it one more try. After all, it was a lovely place.

On the first day, I made a fatal error by claiming to have done the beginners' course, and was put into the intermediate group. Serve me right. The group leader was, oh Lord, please, no, the dreadful Petra, whose eyes narrowed in scorn as soon as she spotted me. Instead of starting off with something easy, she packed us onto a bus and took us to a steep and dangerous-looking hill, which we were to ski down while she assessed our level of ability. I lurked at the back of the group as, one after the other, they ski-ed down the slope with uniform success.

Finally, I was the last person left and could procrastinate no more. I had been told that, like riding a bicycle, you never forget how to do a *Schneepflug*. This was a lie. After a couple of metres, I realised that I was completely out of control. My legs parted in a spectacularly painful splits and I tumbled head over heels all the way down to where my startled classmates waited for me. My skis and poles had all got lost en route and I had an agonising pain in my knee.

"Bollocks to this," I said, retrieved my bits and pieces and limped away back to the bus stop. Without saying goodbye, I returned to the flat to spend the rest of the week brushing up on my by now unrivalled in-depth knowledge of Austrian daytime quiz shows. It took six whole months and intensive physiotherapy before my knee recovered.

So there we were. I admitted that I was temperamentally unsuited to ski-ing (the number one requirement, courage, was missing). Birgit toddled along, better than me, but not really making much progress (at least when sober). And, at the end-of-the-week races, both the children came last.

We never went back to Ramsau.

***

Apart from CFHs, there's another type of holiday one is supposed to indulge in: the Weekend Break. Normally, these are mini-packages to places like Paris or Brussels, and thus to be held in contempt. But I had a better idea. What about an independently self-arranged weekend in Poland?

It wasn't as daft as it sounds. Abandoning children, Birgit and I flew to Warsaw, then caught a train to the eternally fascinating city of Krakow. But that wasn't enough, oh no. Krakow contained UK tourists who had got there by plane. I therefore insisted that we should board a long-distance bus to Zacapone, the "Jewel of the Tatra Mountains".

So, what memories do we cherish of Poland? One above all, and that is its inimitable toilets.

To be fair, we had been warned. "When in Poland", the guide book said," be prepared for the public toilets to be challenging." Snort. For veterans of the original, now fast-disappearing, French "flush-and-run" specials, what possible terrors could Poland's conveniences hold?

One thing is for sure, you can't avoid them, unless you're teetotal. The seductive nature of the extremely strong and outrageously cheap and aptly-named beer, *piwo* (pronounced pee-voh) means that frequent visits are essential.

It was Birgit who alerted me to possible problems. Disappearing into the depths of the cellar of the central arcade in the *"Reynek"* (marketplace) in Krakow, she took a worryingly long time to reappear. It transpired that, after a lengthy queuing procedure, she had been severely told off by the *babcia klazetowa* (brutal old lady in charge of handing out the regulation two sheets of toilet paper). My wife had had the temerity to protest (via sign language) that this wasn't much of a deal for 40 groszy (about 7p). But the main hold-up had been caused by a fruitless search for a flushing mechanism and a fear of the *babcia klazetowa's* reaction if she re-emerged without having flushed. It was only after finally giving up hope that she discovered that the mechanism was in fact activated by opening the door.

A couple of *piwos* later, I had no choice but to follow. Sure enough, I promptly had a run-in with the *babcia klazetowa*, who tried to claim that I had performed a function other than the one I claimed. You see, a pee costs 40 groszy. Something more substantial costs 50 groszy. On this occasion, I was accused of trying to get away cheaply, despite the fact that her beady eye had been on me throughout the operation.

What happened at the gloriously down-at-heel Hotel Dom Turysty in Zacopane (unwelcome memories of Youth Hostels of the past) was, however, beyond a joke. Taken short (50 groszys worth) in the breakfast room, I wrongly assumed that the hotel's facilities would be free. I had already entered the loo when I realised that I had no money.

Pounced upon by the duty crone, who thought I had done the business and was trying to leave without paying, I had to suffer a tirade of abuse as I tried to explain that I was just going back to fetch some coins.

On returning, I offered the 50 groszy I had borrowed, which were quickly pocketed. Unfortunately, the old woman considered that sum to be in payment of my (alleged) previous visit, and now refused to let me in again. When all pleading failed, I had no choice but to return to the breakfast room yet again to procure another 50 groszy. This gained me admission to the cublicle, but in the kerfuffle, the crone hadn't given me my entitlement of two sheets of loo paper, something which I only realised when I physically required it. A furtive peer out of the cubicle door revealed that she had now gone off for a break. The only way to get some paper was to hop, trousers round ankles, from my cubicle to the attendant's kiosk and help myself.

I doubt that the two Dutch backpackers who witnessed this event will ever get over the trauma.

***

Having established that Weekend Breaks are a Good Thing, I then decided to take my friend David to Amsterdam. David is one of those saintly people who selflessly devote their lives to doing good turns for others, while seldom giving a thought to themselves. He works all the time and never even seems to have time for a single day off, far less a Weekend Break. So, when we realised that he was about to celebrate a landmark birthday (probably by spending the entire day staring into a computer screen), we decided to force him to go away for a couple of days.

Actually, it was Birgit's idea. She's full of them. She was leafing through the Travel section of the Sunday paper (as one does) and came across an advert for cheap flights. "Why not take him to Amsterdam for the weekend?"

When you ring up those cheapo travel companies, they make the process so smooth that you've booked before you realise what you're doing. Within moments, the flights had been reserved and paid for. All that was needed now was a hotel, and that also was arranged in a trice by a friend of mine who was working in Amsterdam at the time. He booked us into the Bridge Hotel, a smart but inexpensive establishment in a prime position on the bank of the Amstel.

Within minutes of the birthday card containing the ticket being handed over, the phone lines of Winchester were buzzing.

"I hear you and David are going to Amsterdam for the weekend ..."

"Yes."

"Ho ho, say no more, know what I mean, etc."

"What?"

"Well you know what Amsterdam's famous for, don't you?"

"Er .. canals? Tulips?"

"Come on, Oliver, you're going for the dope and the red light district, aren't you?"

Considering that neither of these things had even entered my head, it came as something of a shock to realise that these are the only two things for which Amsterdam is famous ... even among its own population.

But first, there was the little matter of checking into the hotel. The receptionist, who, along with everyone else in this most cosmopolitan of cities, spoke perfect English, directed us to a room on the first floor. In a disturbing mirror image of the Romantic Weekend in Venice with my wife I'd once arranged, contriving to book a less than Romantic room with two small single beds, the room in the Bridge Hotel contained only a double one.

When I returned to point out that I had requested a room with two single beds, not a double one, the receptionist smiled ruefully: "Well, I did wonder," she said, "but, you know, Amsterdam is that kind of city." She explained the situation in Dutch to the cleaning lady, who could not contain her mirth.

"*Twee Männe!*" she guffawed.

"Yes," I responded, "but not *twee* that particular kind of *Männe.*" Not that anything was of avail, since the hotel was fully booked.

I hadn't shared a bed with anyone but my wife for twenty-odd years, and she tells me I snore, fart and shout out swearwords in my sleep, as well as travelling, crab like, from one side of the double bed to the other in the course of the night. David and I, who are very good friends, but not **that** good, crept into the respective outer limits of the bed and concentrated on not doing any of the above things. Even friendship has its limits.

In my dream, two beautiful Indonesian girls entered the room and insisted on taking me and David out on a tour of the city. But it was only a dream.

In the morning, we asked the receptionist about hiring bicycles.

"Good idea," she said. "You will be able to visit the red light district and ... "(conspiratorial leer) "... the Coffee Shops."

"Well, actually, we were planning to go to the Vondelpark and the Flower Market."

"Yes, but I'm sure you will want to visit the red light area and the ... " (leer Part 2) "... Coffee Shops on the way."

In the bike hire place, it was even worse. The assistant was a real live wire. "You don't want extra insurance? But you will be leaving the bikes in dangerous areas and you ..." - he turned specifically to me, God knows why - "especially **you**, will be going to the Coffee Shops. After that, you will probably have an accident."

Rather pompously, and probably also out of general timidity, we indeed did avoid those famous areas, until tempted into a canalside café called, appropriately in view of the way the city works, "Chaos Café". There we threw caution to the winds and started drinking beer. Prior to that, we had decided that the combination of alcohol and brakeless bikes in a frantic and almost completely anarchic traffic environment could well be lethal. The Heineken they served was pleasingly weak and we soon got talking to the charming barmaid and her equally charming friend.

"Have you been to the red light district yet?"

"No, we thought it might be a bit dangerous."

"Oh no, everything is very calm, because of all the Coffee Shops. You must have visited the Coffee Shops?"

"Well ..." We looked at each other.

"Not yet," I said, " but we plan to visit the red light district and the Coffee Shops this afternoon."

Finally, we had come to realise that the recommendations were genuine and not necessarily an oblique and uncomplimentary inference that we looked like drug-addled dirty old men (even though we undoubtedly did).

"Right, that's it," I thought, "I am bloody well going to go into all the porn shops and I am bloody well going to have a joint."

And so it bloody well transpired, the latter being planned first in order to provide courage for the former.

I remember absolutely everything about the Sixties. It's probably pretty pathetic to admit to waiting until the age of fifty before trying one's first joint. By all accounts, this rite of passage nowadays normally occurs in the primary school playground. But that's the way it was. For goodness sake, I thought, if half the Tory cabinet has tried cannabis, surely it's something you should do before you die? Not that copying the Tory cabinet is anything I'd want to do in any other respect.

This is what happens when you realise that you have scaled the hill of life and are beginning to slide down the other side. But it still didn't stop us worrying about what people would think. The fact that the people of Amsterdam didn't know us, didn't care about us, wouldn't notice us and would never see us again was immaterial.

So there were two humiliating false starts. In the first café we entered, neither of us had the courage to ask for anything other than a beer. The second one turned out to be a cyber café. This was even worse. Before we knew what was happening, we had booked ourselves twenty minutes of computer time as a displacement activity. We thought of sending e-mails to our friends, before realising that we only knew our own addresses and abjectly sending messages to ourselves, to be picked up when we got home: "Wow, look, there's an e-mail from me!"

The third café looked more promising. There were large murals of Bob Marley and reggae music boomed from its murky interior. David ordered something called "space cake" but I was hyper by then and pointed to a box of joints. Sensing my inexperience, the barman looked at me quizzically:

"Is this the first time you smoke?"

I nodded sheepishly.

"Be careful," he warned. "It is very strong, very very strong."

Needless to say, neither of us felt anything whatsoever. We both concluded that the coffee shop was a complete scam. After all, you're hardly likely to go to the police and complain about the poor quality of the drugs, are you?

"I've had enough of this," said David. "I'm buying a bottle of wine."

The Red Light district was marginally more interesting. Certainly, the display of baffling devices was comprehensive, as were the wall-to-wall video cassettes with unlikely-sounding titles. My favourite was called "A Mother, a Daughter, a Fat Woman and a Dog". To judge by the cover photo, the title was a literal rather than a metaphorical description. But, after a while, we realised that all the shops were duplicating themselves and that most were obviously part of a chain. As, shockingly, were the "Bob Marley" Coffee Shops. There were loads of them, all with identical décor.

We then had to come to terms with the upsetting fact that the Ladies of the Night were mass-produced as well. Each one was presented in a little cabin, rather like in Hamburg, where I'd been amazed and thrilled to find that all the prostitutes looked like supermodels and not at all like the pock-marked, syphilis-ridden Dickensian hags that the term conjured up in my mind. But the ladies of Amsterdam were disappointingly unalluring and, once you'd noticed that most of them had positioned several rolls of kitchen towel beside their couches (oh God!), not in the least bit tempting. Still, one of them actually did utter to me the immortal words, "Hi there, big boy". How did she know?

After that, the touristy things we did were less daring but more satisfying. We went the whole hog with a full-scale vegetarian Indonesian *Rejstafel*, quite an experience because it was so spicy that it rendered both of us completely unable to speak for nearly an hour. Then we spent a wild and wonderful evening in the Melkweg, a brilliant music venue where we saw a reassuringly wholesome and ultra-funky New York girl band called Luscious Jackson.

We must have looked like a couple of homeless beggars when, after the concert, we sat on a bench on a bridge over the Amstel and desperately tried to get high. I had kept the stub of my joint in my trouser pocket, but when I tried to retrieve it, I found that it had disintegrated. I sniffed hoplessly at the debris until David fished out the remains of his bottle of wine and we shared it, before retiring to the luxury of our new, non-double-bedded room.

So I'm still yet ever to get high. I don't know if that's something to be proud of or ashamed of.

In the morning, we hired a small electric boat to ply the canals. Three charming girls, in charge of the boats, recommended us a good route.

"You will pass through the red light district and the area of the Coffee Shops," they said.

"Oh no we won't," we replied.

Chapter 13.

Lone Star

Polly Harvey and John Parish wrote an immortal song called "Why D'Ya Go To Cleveland?" In the chorus, it enquires, gently, "Why D'Ya Have To Go Down There?"

That was the question we were asked again and again before, during and after our visit to Austin, Texas: "Why?" Back then, in 1999, it didn't even have the distinction of being known as George W. Bush land, because, well, nobody knew much about George W. Bush. But I knew all about Austin, oh yes.

Down in Southampton, there's a music club called The Brook. There I had seen artists such as Omar and the Howlers, Joe Ely and Bobby Mack. What they all had in common was that they all came from Texas and they all shared a thwacking R & B style after the fashion of Austin's acknowledged hero Stevie Ray Vaughan. Apart, that is, from poor Bobby Mack, who complained that he couldn't get a gig in Austin.

Couldn't get a gig in Austin? How so? Austin is the self-styled but also unassailed Live Music Capital of the World. It is a city which contains hundreds of live music venues, far more per square mile than anywhere else on the planet. If a fine guitar player such as Bobby Mack couldn't get a gig there, then what must the quality control be like? Certainly nothing like Ye Olde Sticky Carpette in London's Camden, where anyone can walk in off the street with a guitar and an amp and be allowed to play.

So, when I needed a special treat, I requested a trip to Austin. I was worried, I'll admit it. The "Why?" definitely seemed to suggest that Austin must be grotty by day and of no interest to anyone not into music. Was it going to be unsuitable as a holiday destination, as opposed to a research object or an anorak's delight?

We arrived at Houston airport and suffered an immediate embarrassment when we couldn't start the hire car. Apparently, you can't start an automatic when it's in gear, but how were we to know that?

As we cruised the highway (that sounds so great, I'll say it again: cruised the highway) towards Austin, I imagined a road movie-style motel rearing up out of the heat haze, where we would chew the fat with the local cowboys and stick a dime into the jukebox. However, the perfect motel somehow never seemed to appear, so Birgit just had to keep driving ... and driving ... and driving. The problem was that she was severely jetlagged and getting more and more tired. As her eyelids began to droop irrevocably, there was good news: Austin City Limits.

I took out the map of the city and tried to orientate myself. It seemed perfectly straighforward. We were on the main Houston to Austin Highway, and to either side stretched the various roads: First Street, Second Street, Third Street, etc. How simple. All we had to do was drive down one of these and there was bound to be a hotel where we could stay. The only trouble was that we were up in the air on an elevated freeway, while the roads on the map were down below. As I haplessly tried to interpret the map, the trouble started.

We descended on a slip road, but before we knew it, we found ourselves heading off back down the freeway towards Houston. The exhausted Birgit was beginning to get angry. Off we came again, only to disappear into a massive trading estate full of warehouses, fast food outlets, furniture stores but no hotels. Back onto the freeway, off it again, down a few dead ends, onto another freeway heading towards Dallas, off it again ...

Suddenly, as in a scene from a movie, Birgit pulled onto the sidewalk, threw open the door, tossed the keys into my lap, shouted, "That's it, you can bloody drive yourself, I've had enough!", slammed the door shut again and took off down the road.

Phew! I love you when you're angry! This was quite a sensational moment, not at all the way she normally behaves, but pretty damn impressive. People always do that in road movies, don't they? How authentic! But, as you know, I have a driving phobia, so there was nothing for it but to trot off down the road after her, gesticulating, grovellingly apologising for my uselessness and begging for clemency. "I'll pay for us to stay in the smartest hotel in town," I heard myself saying, unconvincingly.

"Sod off. I don't want the smartest hotel, I want the nearest hotel, you idiot."

The nearest hotel turned out to be just round the corner. It only had a Smoking room left, but Birgit was beyond caring and I was beyond daring. She collapsed onto the bed and passed out, but something peculiar had happened to me. I was wide awake and raring to check out this paradise I'd come so far to experience. Oh, and there was another thing.

In the plane on the way over, I'd been reading the biography of Billy Bragg. This singer and songwriter appeals to me in the way that Tony Benn and Ken Livingstone do, in that he is a realistic socialist whose every word seems to make total sense. Plus, he has a perhaps unexpectedly well-developed sense of humour.

The biography revealed that Billy had bought a house just along the coast from my favourite place in the whole world (see the Epilogue). On my headphones, I was listening to a brilliant album that Billy had made with an American country band called Wilco, re-interpreting the songs of Woody Guthrie. But, as I listened, something even more remarkable happened. The airline magazine had a section on Austin, which revealed that Billy Bragg was appearing that very day, at somewhere called Waterloo.

Probably my only positive characteristic is determination to carry out tasks which I set myself. And there, on the plane, I had set myself the task of seeing Billy Bragg at Waterloo in Austin, Texas. I could not possibly imagine anything better. And I couldn't imagine not achieving it.

It was mid-evening and the heat was stifling as I strode down the steep hill towards Sixth Street. In the distance, sounds were becoming apparent ... the thwack of a snare drum, the rumble of a bass, the chunky chiming of a Telecaster. But then, there seemed to be more than one of each, coming from all directions. As I reached Sixth, I realised that the myth was, in fact, reality: Every building in the street was a bar, and every bar had a band playing in it.

Admittedly, I was jet-lagged, but I wasn't on drugs. I have never felt as wonderful as I did in that moment. If you can't relate to music, it doesn't matter. Just think of your favourite thing in the world, be it art, literature, sport, food, religion or whatever, then imagine yourself completely surrounded by it. There, doesn't that feel good?

On the corner was a brightly-lit bar. The band was taking a break, so I approached the girl who was serving:

"Excuse me, do you know where Billy Bragg is playing?"

"Who?"

"Billy Bragg."

"Just a moment ... Wayne, do you know where Bobby Bland is playing?"

"No, no ... hang on ... How can I get to Waterloo?"

"Oh, that's easy. Just keep on walking down Sixth and you'll get there soon enough."

It was eleven o' clock at night but something like five in the morning for me. I didn't care. On and on I walked, occasionally stopping to get a reassuring "Just keep right on walking", until, after at least three miles, I saw a neon sign at the top of a hill. This was it!

Except that it wasn't. Waterloo turned out to be a record shop, not a club. What was more, Billy Bragg had been there at lunchtime, merely performing a couple of songs and doing a CD signing session. And none of the staff seemed remotely interested in either Billy or his work. Still, the journey hadn't been wasted. I felt that I had done my duty, so bought a couple of CDs and set off back the way I had come. On the return journey, I visited five bars, had five beers, heard five bands and ate the most heavenly hamburger of my life, all at breakfast time. No way could life get any better.

During the next few days, we found that just wandering was a fine occupation in Austin. Mainly because the University of Texas campus is so gigantic and the population so youthful, it is one of the USA's least threatening cities. Laid out on hills of almost San Franciscan gradients, it nevertheless boasts fine facilities for cyclists and skateboarders and a comprehensive bus system.

Most appealingly, we found that it had a number of large urban parks. One of these surrounded the newly-restored State Capitol, a beautiful white, domed building from where the state of Texas is governed. It was worth entering just for a cool-down. When we were in Austin, the outside temperature was 95 degrees and walking into the State Capitol was literally like leaping from a sauna into the splashpool (except that, thankfully, everyone kept their clothes on). Spurning the guided tour (obviously), it was still worth looking at the preserved Treasurer's Office and trying out the startling amplifying effect of speaking below the four-floor high dome. Most sounds in Austin are amplified ones.

On a hillside just outside the city centre, we found Zilker Park, a joyous destination on a hot day because of its freshwater spring-fed lake, Barton Springs. For a mere three bucks (it would have been nothing at all if we had got there early enough) we could spend the day slipping in and out of the crystal-clear 68 degree waters and soaking up the sun on the grass slopes. Most of the clientèle was exquisitely tattooed and comprehensively body-pierced, so our lily-white British hue elicited plenty of "Why Austin?"s and much in the way of friendly and welcoming banter. Afterwards, we sauntered through the Botanical gardens and took a ride on the Zilker Zephyr miniature railway.

After leaving the emergency hotel, the accommodation we found was mind-bogglingly good. Asking in the Visitor Centre for a B & B, we were a little startled by the price. "In Texas," explained the assistant, "Bed and Breakfast is not the same as in the UK. The host family views it as a privilege to have you in their house."

It was almost humblingly good, since the annexe we were allotted turned out to be a separate colonial-style house, complete with its own veranda and rocking chair, a huge fan-cooled sitting room, a large kitchen with a fully-stocked "help yourself to ice cream" fridge-freezer and a bedroom of unparalleled luxury - all for the price of a standard motel. Breakfast was a gourmet feast of fresh fruit and a different speciality delight each day, including home-made spinach quiche and "Texan Egg Florets" - poached eggs and herbs in a choux pastry basket.

So, about that music ... How could it have disappointed? The only problem lay in deciding which bars to enter and how long to stay. You could ply Sixth for weeks before repeating yourself, but we found that it was best to be adventurous, stick a pin in the huge listings guide and take a flyer on someone you hadn't heard of. One thing was for sure, you weren't going to be disappointed by the quality.

The premier club in Austin is Antone's, a huge blues cavern. It was so full that they had set up little satellite bars on wheels out in the audience to relieve the crush at the main bars (which you couldn't reach anyway). These fairy-light-adorned bathtubs full of ice and bottled beer rapidly sold out and had to be frequently replenished. We caught the third night in an annual four-night residency by the legendary James Brown saxist Maceo Parker and his impossibly funky band. According to the people we talked to, the whole of Austin looks forward to Maceo's visits, which explained why the eighty-dollar tickets were so hard to come by.

As we queued, the band rolled up outside the club in a fleet of limos with darkened windows. We danced until 2 am before retiring in exhaustion while Maceo played on. As with everywhere we went, we made friends instantly, always based on the inevitable "Why Austin?". In this case, the reply was easy: "Just look around you. Isn't it bloody obvious?"

It would be easy to drone on about all the rest of the music, but even non-music freaks should visit Austin for the stunningly beautiful surrounding countryside. We found a quick way to sample its appeal by taking a half-hour drive out to the Austinites' favourite excursion destination, the Oasis on Lake Travis. This precariously-perched eight-storey wooden hillside construction houses a whole range of restaurants and bars from which we could peer over the balcony railing (28 decks, 450 feet above the water) and savour what was claimed to be the world's most spectacular sunset (I wouldn't argue, but then I haven't been everywhere in the world), whilst dining surprisingly reasonably.

Hill Country is LBJ country and only an hour's drive from Austin, we came across the exaggeratedly named Johnson City (a crossroads and a few shacks). The LBJ State Park, however, was really worth a visit, containing a nicely understated visitor centre and a fully-working turn-of-the-century cattle ranch where we were able to commune with the turkeys and the Longhorns and even help a costumed "Momma" to prepare a full-scale authentic lunch for the hungry cowboys. Just up the road, Lady Bird Johnson still resides, taking care of the Texas wild flowers which she has apparently made her responsibility.

Passing through Stonewall, where every roadside farm and shack was selling peaches, peach jam, peach juice and peach ice-cream, we came, totally unprepared, to what must surely be Hill Country's strangest and most alluring town, Fredericksburg. As we drove along the main street, something seemed strange. Shops were called things like *"Bäckerei"* and *"Metzgerei"*. The German settlers who arrived here in 1846 created a completely German environment and every shop in Fredericksburg has a German name, most of the signs are in German and there's even a German brewery and a *"Weihnachtsmarkt"*.

The only un-German thing was the heat. The way the wooden buildings stretched out along either side of the highway made Fredericksburg genuinely feel as if, at any moment, a cowboy was going to ride into town, hitch his horse up to the saloon and burst through the swing doors for a shootout.

This feeling intensified seventeen miles into the wilderness as we rounded a bend to gasp at the splendour of Enchanted Rock. This huge, bare, red granite hill is straight out of your favourite Western, and the one-mile struggle to the top was worth every pant. The infinite views in all directions were incomparable and, this being Commanche country, we expected, at any second, a feathered headdress to appear over the brow, between the cactuses. The only trouble was that it was impossible to sit down at the top, since the rock was literally red-hot. Apparently, it groans as it cools down in the evening, leading the Red Indians to attribute magical powers to it. As usual, we were instantly befriended by the only other tourists there, only this time they had no need to ask "Why?"

From Fredericksburg it was only a further hour's drive to San Antonio and the Alamo.

Now this was an important visit for me, because, when I was a schoolboy, I had gone to immense trouble to obtain a Davy Crockett hat by collecting hundreds of tokens from tins of Armour Star provisions. All our friends, neighbours and relations had to chew their way through untold amounts of corned beef, peach slices and pineapple chunks to assist me in that quest.

When the desired object finally arrived, it was rather a disappointment. Far from being manufactured from raccoon skin, it was made of some kind of synthetic fibre and I looked as if I had a cat sitting on my head. Besides, I shared none of the gnarled, weatherbeaten machismo of Fess Parker, and, worst of all, the Davy Crockett phase had passed and been replaced by something else. I never wore my Davy Crockett hat and the many indigestion-suffering people who had helped me were not at all pleased.

Nonetheless, the Alamo was obviously a must-see. When we'd got over the surprise that the edifice is now slap-bang in the centre of the city, the visit was hugely rewarding, especially as we had had time to view the 40-minute, pleasingly unsentimental "Alamo - The Price of Freedom" on the huge adjacent IMAX screen. So tasteful was this film that we felt genuinely humble when entering the shrine itself, where the excellently low-key museum offered hours of fascination with details of the battle and artefacts such as James Bowie's knife and David Crockett's razor.

Before leaving San Antonio, we strolled down River Walk, in two minds as to whether to love or hate it. After disastrous floods in the 1920s, the San Antonio River was incorporated into the city reconstruction, so that we had the feeling that we were in a kind of sub-tropical cross between a shopping mall and Venice. In the end, we decided to love it (that was the effect that Texas was having on us) and abandoned ourselves to a crayfish extravaganza in one of the waterside restaurants with ludicrously cheap "Happy Hour" offers.

Back in Austin, the old problem raised itself: So many venues, so little time. Pin-sticking proved triumphant once more, as the unpromising-sounding Monte Montgomery at the even less enticing-sounding Saxon Pub, turned out to be a feast of brilliant self-penned acoustic country-rock in a classic Texas roadhouse setting. We banged down a few Tequilas, bought his album and shouted "Yeah!' a lot.

***

Part Two of the musical odyssey was to take place in New Orleans. Flying in from Houston, we immediately became involved in a classic American situation (or at least how you imagine such a thing to be). At New Orleans airport, we stood in a queue for a taxi and soon found ourselves in a minibus, along with several other baffled passengers. It said Taxi on it, but one essential element of a taxi, the surly, taciturn driver, was missing.

"Well, hi there, folks," boomed a crackly voice over the deafening PA, "my name's Bob and I'm your host for today. I'd like to welcome you folks to my home city of New Orleans and as we go along, I'll be telling you all about the history of this fine city of ours."

We hadn't asked for a guided tour and didn't particularly want one, but Bob's tour was actually pretty interesting, if rather verbose. He told us about the history of slavery, the plantations, the Cajun music and food, and how the graves in New Orleans are above the ground rather than below it, in order to prevent the bodies from floating to the surface.

But I knew what was going to happen. Bob took us round several hotels, dropping off passengers en route, until Birgit and I were the only ones left in the minibus. As he drew up outside the Days Inn, he ran round, opened the door, helped Birgit out, insisted on grabbing the luggage and generally notched his level of obsequiousness up to new heights.

"Well, folks - what were your names again? - I sure hope you enjoyed your little tour and this is your host Bob signing off and saying 'bye for now."

In my wallet, I had just one fifty dollar bill left until I could get to the next ATM machine.

"How much do we owe you, Bob?"

"Fifty dollars."

I gave him the note and showed him my empty wallet.

"I'm really sorry, Bob, but that's all I've got. We really enjoyed the tour, but we can't give you a tip."

Instantly, his face changed from that of genial host to a mask of fury and hatred.

"You motherfucking sonofabitch, you think I'm going to waste my breath giving you a tour of the city and you're not going to give me a fucking tip? Hasn't this woman of yours got any money?"

"No, because we've just flown in and haven't had the chance ..."

"Well, I'll be goddamned."

For a moment, I wondered whether he was going to pull a gun and frogmarch me to the nearest cash machine, but in the end, he jumped back into his bus and accelerated away, still yelling, cursing and gesticulating out of the window. I'm sure I heard the words "cocksuckin' Limeys" at one stage.

Of all the things you have to get used to in the States, the principal one is remembering that any price you see will have a hefty percentage of tax added to it (varying from state to state). The other is not to be offended by the "tip culture". Anyone who serves you in any way will be extremely friendly and helpful, and will expect to be tipped.

There are plenty of people who will tell you that Americans are superficial and insincere, that all that "Y'all have a nice day now" stuff is cringe-makingly bland. Well, I'm here to tell you that these are the attitudes of sour-faced Brits who, as a result, receive the crap levels of service and the poor standards of communication they deserve. If someone welcomes me to their town and wishes me a nice day, I'm delighted. If I'd had any money, I'd have tipped Bob with the greatest of pleasure.

The implication that the only reason that people in America are nice to you is in order to profit from you is cynical in the extreme (okay, so maybe Bob was an exception). What about all the people who are nice to you simply because they are friendly and communicative and like to welcome strangers, and who couldn't profit from you in any way? Eh?

Anyway, even if that is the motive, I don't care. I'd far rather have someone being insincerely nice to me than negative and suspicious. Which is a good reason for liking all of America except possibly New York, where, for some reason, everyone is brusque, loud and in a frantic hurry.

In New Orleans, the guidebooks tell you, rather schizophrenically, to explore areas other than the French Quarter and Bourbon Street, while at the same time warning of the danger of getting too far off the beaten track. Some of the highly-recommended music clubs are located in the very areas you are advised to approach with caution. So we did something which was really successful: We took a streetcar and followed its route from start to terminus, thus getting a real feel for a whole range of different areas.

Bourbon Street really is something else. Out of every bar blasts Cajun music of wildly varying quality and, of course, you have to try the gumbo and all the various types of Cajun food. This we did on a balcony overlooking a seedy sex bar. It was hilarious to watch the tourists studying the posters outside, which described in lurid detail the forbidden delights within. Five minutes later, they would emerge with expressions of resentful disappointment on their faces; whoops, they'd been had.

The French Quarter truly revels in its status as the only place in the US where there's no law against drinking liquor in the street. Every doorway contains a little man or woman with a barrel of beer, selling you "Bud to Go" or "Dollar Bud" in a plastic cup. That is fantastic value, so fantastic, in fact, that it's probably watered down (it certainly tasted that way). But that is advantageous anyway, because you can drink loads of it without ever getting over-drunk.

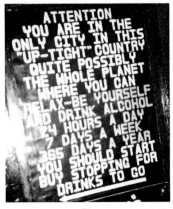

Sic.

There was a big football match in town the weekend we arrived in New Orleans, so the streets in the French Quarter were even fuller than usual. It was like the Glastonbury Festival when they've inadvertently allowed 20,000 extra people to climb in over the fence. You could only progress extremely slowly, taking care not to stumble and not even thinking of overtaking or changing direction. And every single person, young, old, male, female, carried a little plastic beaker of Bud.

We had absolutely no qualms about being tourists and doing all the tourist things (hey, I'm getting mellow in my old age, okay?), so we shamelessly paced the shopping malls of the waterfront, took a paddle steamer cruise with the legendary Dukes of Dixieland, and then patronised the House of Blues. All right, this was a bit plastic, along the lines of the Hard Rock Café, but with magnificent music courtesy of the aged and authentic R.L. Burnside, and with busts of all the blues greats set into the ceiling of the dining room. The only problem was that it was hard to concentrate on what was on your plate while trying to identify who in the firmament was who. Okay, that's got to be Buddy Guy, but surely that's not Jeff Beck? Bloody hell, it is!

So often, something that appears attractive in a glossy colour brochure turns out to be a rip-off, so we had no particular hopes, as we booked ourselves onto a Louisiana Swamp Tour. Again, a minibus collected us from the hotel (my blood ran cold as I checked to see who was driving, but it was okay). The affable driver repeated all the stuff that Bob had told us the day before, but gradually we were away from the city and driving through increasingly sinister-looking swamplands. We ended up in a place which, far from being glossy, was some kind of tumbledown trailer park.

With just four other tourists, we boarded a flat-bottomed boat called "Swamp Thing" and immediately realised that this was to be no rip-off bit of tourist exploitation. The skipper explained how his family had lived on the swamp for generations and pointed out how all the houses were on stilts and how several of them were currently roofless on account of the recent tail end of a hurricane which had passed through. Just like the African Queen, the boat glided through shady glades and endless swamplands, occasionally startling the odd dozing armadillo into action along the banks.

Eventually, we arrived in a small clearing and the engine was switched off. The captain started calling *"Viens ici, viens ici!"* and tossing marshmallows, apparently the preferred treat of alligators, into the water.

Oh yeah, I thought, this will never work. But I was quite wrong. We waited for a few moments in a total silence only punctuated by the occasional shout of *"Viens ici!"* before, suddenly, with a resounding snap, one of the marshmallows was gone. And then another, and another. All around us, pairs of dark but very alert eyes stared from the surface of the water.

What then followed was, I suppose, a bit like a dolphin show, except that this was in a clearing in a swamp in the back of beyond, and was genuine rather than staged. We were allowed to dangle bits of meat on the end of a pole to tempt the alligators to leap up and grab them (which they did, spectacularly). Then the skipper frightened the lives out of us by producing, from a bucket in the cabin, a genuine baby alligator called Elvis, which we were invited to hold.

That Marshmallow Moment

As we continued on our way, we emerged onto a huge lake, dotted with a few small islands and a number of electric pylons. As we tourists sat and nattered about our experiences, there was a sudden change of atmosphere. In the space of about thirty seconds, the light went from bright sunshine to almost pitch black. "Uh-oh," said the captain, "there's another sting in that hurricane's tail coming up", and revved up the engine, obviously aware that the weather was capable of changing in moments.

Initially, I think, he planned to head for home, but before we could make any progress, the storm-force wind and sheeting rain had arrived, reducing visibility to nothing. The flat-bottomed boat (built that way because of the shallowness of the bayous) had no stability and was being literally tossed about like that proverbial cork we hear so much about. I was vaguely aware of one of the electric pylons rearing up out of the darkness and passing by with just millimetres to spare.

We passengers cowered in a huddle in the middle of the boat. I do remember vaguely thinking that perhaps this sort of thing was commonplace and that our skipper would be casually treating it as an everyday event. I looked towards his little cockpit and was quickly disabused of my comforting thought. He was as white as a sheet, his face a mixture of terror and confusion as he struggled to keep hold of the wheel. This was the real thing all right.

I remember trying to be jolly and shouting into Birgit's ear,

"Never mind, at least the water isn't cold."

She mouthed something at me.

"What?"

"Alligators!"

Shit, somehow I'd forgotten the alligators.

What strange thoughts we have at times of stress. I genuinely recall thinking, yes, we're going to die, but hey, what a spectacular way to go! At the same time, I worried about the children having to spend the rest of their lives explaining to people that their parents had been eaten alive by 'gators.

With a sickening thud (I know thuds are always sickening, but I've never felt sicker, I can tell you), we crashed headlong into one of the islands, and were instructed to grab hold of tree branches and hold on for dear life. Just adjacent to us was yet another pylon. The captain explained that, far from being an accident, he had actually intended to hit the island, in an effort to find some shelter. And indeed, the island did seem to offer some protection as the storm passed by, as swiftly as it had arrived.

On the way back to base, the skipper unconvincingly tried to give the impression that he hadn't been worried at all. But, as we sat drinking a much-needed beer afterwards, I overheard him telling a colleague that, in thirty years of running swamp tours, that had been the worst storm he had ever encountered.

Before leaving New Orleans, there was one more thing we had to do. Every few yards down Bourbon Street, there were table dancing clubs, and I decided I had to go to one. After all, it was something I'd never experienced, and this seemed the perfect place to do it. But how do you tell your wife that you want to go and watch nubile young girls cavorting, more or less naked, on a table?

In the end, I just asked. Birgit, as usual, was completely unfazed and simply said, what a good idea. But then our abject ignorance came into play. We both knew that there are certain places in particular areas in Hamburg where, if any woman were unwittingly to venture, she'd be likely to end up with a bucket of slops being poured over her head. So we picked a reasonably salubrious-looking club and studied the entrance for a while. In fact, at least half the clients seemed to be couples, so we enquired about the price and entered. Inside, it wasn't much different from a plushy disco. Even the drinks prices, while not cheap, were tolerable.

This daring adventure was a complete success. What takes some getting used to is the concept of staring at semi-naked women without getting your face slapped, but having once accepted that that is what they are there for, you realise that it would, in fact, be rather insulting not to stare at them. The atmosphere was actually rather wholesome, almost like being in a rather noisy museum. Okay, they were stripping, but not teasing, in that they had very few clothes on in the first place and whipped them off in a trice.

There were other attractions, too, such as the redneck cowboys who paid extra for favoured girls to come along, plonk down a stool in front of them and treat them to a personal show, amid much whistling, slapping of thighs and calls of "Yee-haa!". Or the fact that, the second Birgit went to the loo, several girls immediately approached me, thinking I was on my own, and asked if I'd like them to dance for me. Oh, and since you ask, yes, there was indeed a "back room", into which girls and clients would periodically disappear.

I recommend going to a lap dancing club, but I also recommend that, if you do, you go with your wife, husband or partner. It'll make you feel less like a dirty old man / woman.

Well, when we got to the airport, the flight had been overbooked and we couldn't get on the plane, Far from being furious, we were actually quite pleased, because we didn't really want to go home. They put us up in a Holiday Inn, bought us supper and breakfast and upgraded us to first class, complete with leather seats, champers and king prawns. So every cloud has a silver lining, even if it is the tail end of a hurricane.

Chapter 14

Virgin On The Sublime

The thing about steel band music is that it doesn't really have any dynamics. It's very sunny and cheerful, but somehow, it doesn't really move you.

We'd been sitting in the departure lounge at Antigua Airport for about an hour, when something struck me:

"Haven't we heard this song before?"

"Yes, in fact I think we've heard it several times."

This was a bad thing to notice, because it otherwise might have merely drifted by unremarked, like most muzak does. But now that we had realised that it was a tape loop, it became impossible to avoid being irritated by it. And, as it turned out, there were three more hours to go. What was more, when we stopped over on the return journey, it was still going. I'll bet you it's still going right now, at this very moment. If you're reading this in the lounge at Antigua airport, give us a ring to confirm that, will you?

Antigua airport at first seemed quite quaint, after we'd got used to the fact that the beer prices were in Antiguan dollars rather than US ones. For a frightening moment, it had appeared that drinking beer in the Caribbean was going to be as expensive as drinking champagne at the Ritz, in which case I might as well have gone straight home.

As everyone else took their connections and departed, we didn't. But at least the announcements were charmingly matter-of-fact. None of that "operational difficulties" stuff, oh no.

"We regret to announce that LIAT flight number 2244 to Tortola is delayed until further notice because there's something wrong with the plane," said the tannoy.

Every now and then, there would be a variation on the theme:

"There's still something wrong with the plane."

"The engineers are still looking to see what's wrong with the plane."

"The engineers think they've found out what's wrong with the plane and they're going to try and sort it out."

Most of our fellow travellers were obviously regular LIAT customers who didn't seem at all perturbed. In fact, I was pleased to note that not a single one of them looked a bit like a tourist. They all had plenty of ribald things to say about LIAT, though:

"Do you know why the airline is called LIAT?"

"No, why?"

"It stands for Landing In A Tree! Waaaaaaaaaaurgh!!"

"No, no, that's not true. It's Luggage In Another Terminal! Waaaaaaaaaaurgh!!"

I thought I'd join in.

"Lost In Antiguan Territory! Waaaaaaaaaurgh!!"

Silence. Obviously that wasn't funny. Well, it wasn't, but I think more to the point was that it was okay for natives to take the piss out of their airline but not for visitors.

What about some souvenirs? Admittedly, it seemed odd to purchase souvenirs before the holiday had even started, but there wasn't much else to do to pass the time. Antiguan souvenirs, it turned out, are pleasantly well-focussed. There were Viv Richards mugs, Viv Richards calendars, Viv Richards videos, Viv Richards teatowels, Viv Richards umbrellas, Viv Richards caps, Viv Richards T-shirts and Viv Richards condoms. No, I made that one up. Either way, it was damned impressive. That man is truly the King of Antigua, even though his cricketing career is over. But I didn't buy anything.

What exactly am I doing, I wondered? Sitting in a stifling room, the steel drums rattling unmelodically round the inside of my cranium, surrounded by Viv Richards memorabilia, becoming increasingly addled by Carib Beer and reading, for crying out loud, a biography of Ian Dury. I was truly being hit with a rhythm stick.

So what's this all about? Well, rather disappointingly, it's a Happy Ending. Strictly speaking, I'd have preferred not to mention this particular adventure, because it irritatingly messes up the "all holidays are shit" theme. But luckily, the following summer, we did have a horrific fortnight in Germany during which it rained all the time, the sea was polluted and full of glutinous jellyfish and both the children had turned into revolting teenagers (yes, in both senses). So don't worry, it was just a blip.

Birgit and I never had a honeymoon. I think we considered it was a bourgeois convention or something. Or else we couldn't afford one, which is probably more likely. Either way, the trip to the British Virgin Islands was designed to celebrate twenty years of marriage (there's obviously something wrong with us, because nobody else manages that). We set out to prove that the perfect holiday could be achieved, and I was quietly confident that we would be proved entirely wrong.

We found it on the internet. If it had been just me, I'd have literally gone for subsisting in a self-built twig hut on a truly deserted desert island, living on coconuts and boiled slugs, anything to let my misanthropy really run riot. But Birgit is scared of spiders and likes nice beds, so that might have been going a bit far. The homepage for Turtle Dove Cottages looked so idyllic that it seemed really hopeful as a compromise.

We could have been wrong. I mean, bloody Turtle bloody Dove Cottages. Come off it! We've all had enough experience of the way names like that are dished out quite inappropriately in order to give gullible travellers a false impression. "Rose Cottage" next to a six-lane highway in Birmingham, "Blackberry Way" snaking its way through an industrial estate, the Kennet and Avon canal flowing past an atomic power station (blimey, that one's true), you know the kind of thing.

It was almost looking as if we were never going to find out, but eventually the call came: "It's okay, everyone, the engineer's located what was wrong and has fixed it." Bloody well hope he has. Do you think the Caribbean has salt-water alligators?

So it was the middle of the night when we arrived at the tiny airport of Tortola. I almost didn't look at the large yellow banner which greeted passengers as they formed up into the long queue for completing the many formalities required in order to enter the country. Posters for events are always jinxed for me. You can guarantee that the concert by Michael Jackson and Madonna, which took the world by storm, took place the night before we arrived, while the double-header featuring the Rolling Stones and a re-formed Beatles complete with a hologram of John Lennon is scheduled to take place the day after we are committed to depart. So it was up to Birgit to point out,

"Look, it's tomorrow."

"What is?"

"The First-Ever BVI Music Festival."

Sure enough, there it was, in black on yellow: The First-Ever BVI Music Festival, starring Maxi Priest and a cast of thousands, on the beach in Cane Garden Bay, and the date was tomorrow's. Memories of the Billy Bragg fiasco convinced me momentarily that the time difference meant that today was actually yesterday, but it wasn't. Tomorrow really was tomorrow. It must be an omen. Everything was going to go right. And it did.

First, however, we had to get to Turtle Dove Cottages. The owners had Emailed that someone with the disappointingly non-Caribbean name of Dave would pick us up in a taxi. I considered the suggestion rather decadent, but, having been informed that the only alternative would be to walk ten miles across rocky and mountainous terrain with no lights, I conceded that a taxi might, after all, be acceptable.

We fully expected that Dave would be a garrulous person along the lines of the ill-remembered Bob in New Orleans before he turned nasty, and that the music in the taxi would be dub reggae or yet more steel drums. But Dave, having greeted us by unsuccessfully attempting to make a joke which was supposed to appeal to an English guest ("Helleur. Weurd yer lark a cuppa tay?"), didn't say a further word. There was a reason for that.

Out of the radio was pouring more fire and brimstone than surely any god could ever have intended to be poured. Hideous retribution was threatened to us for more or less anything we would dare to think about doing, apart from praying, saying halleluyah or generally grovelling at the feet of the Lord, oh yeah. But it wasn't just an interlude, it was an actual local radio station dedicated to only this. What was more, it was emitting from the dashboard at a louder volume than a Motorhead concert. And that's coming from someone who has (with discomfort) survived several Motorhead concerts. It was unbearable.

Following my customary blind and mistaken adherence to stereotypes, I had assumed that, just because Dave had dreadlocks and a little woolly hat, he must be a pothead who would far rather be listening to the Wailers. I was within a verbal hair's breadth of piping up, "I say, Dave old chap, can't you turn off this load of old bollocks and put on some decent music?" but something restrained me. Just as well. The question actually came out as:

"I say, Dave, this Music Festival looks great, doesn't it? Will you be going?"

"I will not be going to the Music Festival. Music like that is ungodly and heathen and the festival is a disgrace to the island."

With that, he turned up the radio to an even more brutal decibel level and concentrated on ramming his taxi into the vicious speed bumps with an even more coccyx-crunching velocity. That put me in my place then.

Morning at Turtle Dove Cottages. I could tell you about it, but you would die of jealousy, the book dropping from your nerveless fingers. So just think of any hyperbole you have ever read in a holiday brochure on the subjects of brightness of sun, blueness of sea, greenness of vegetation, balminess of air and all that other load of junk which normally isn't true. Except that, on this occasion, it was. And to drone on about the wonderfulness of our Conventional Holiday Activities would make this too much like a picture postcard, so you'll have to imagine them as well.

The cottages were attached by a thread to the side of a rocky precipice overlooking the sea, and approachable only with extreme care and considerable energy up a sheer slope and round a couple of unfenced hairpin bends beyond which lay oblivion. It was obvious that we would have to hire a jeep but we were definitely going to have to avoid drinking and driving.

In the morning, we met the sweet American couple who ran the cottages. They gave us the first clue to something which was going to become more and more depressingly obvious. They were finding it hard to make ends meet because their mainly American clientèle were unwilling to accept the very things which had made us choose them: the natural, individual, non-corporate facilities. For example, there was a power failure almost every day. Big deal, it normally didn't last long and merely meant you might have to have a cold shower or wait a while before having a hot one. Down below, at Long Bay, there was a new "resort" which had its own generator. People, they said, preferred to pay a lot more and have their hot showers instantly.

An hour later, this impression was reinforced. The visitors' book in the cottage gave lots of useful tips about what previous inhabitants had experienced. Number one on the list: You must have breakfast at the Carrot Bay Shell Museum, just a walk down the hillside and along the road.

Egberth Donovan was the proprietor of what must surely be the craziest and most appealing of all restaurants. On the ground floor, populated mainly by free-running bantams and pygmy goats, was the Shell Musem, painstakingly collected and assembled by Egberth's team at night, open to the elements at all hours and carefully packed away in the hurricane season. And, in amongst the shells, hundreds of wooden boards scrawled with words of impenetrable wisdom. Almost all of them exuded a kind of painful sadness, guided, more often than not, by the poverty of the owners and the fear that the days are numbered for their way of life. Oh, plus a few other concerns:

"Satan was so bad in Heaven, God could not take it. If he had shown that demon out, life for some of us would not be so bad."

"Our little island is so pretty that you don't want to leave, then the rain come down."

Egberth cooked us the most ludicrous breakfast of eggs, bacon, bread, pancakes, fruit, fruit juice and unlimited coffee for just five US dollars. It was by far the best breakfast and the best value on the island, yet we were the only customers. The unstoppable Egberth talked for over an hour about his life and the way that he had to work all night as well as all day, taking just two hours' sleep, simply in order to survive. The reason? The newly-arrived "resorts" encouraged their clients never to leave them, offering full board and modern facilities which he could never rival. The writing was on the wall for the Shell Museum and we felt so sad. Here, at least, we had been confident of escaping the claws of multinationalism, but no chance.

Down at Cane Garden Bay, little short of a hallucination was happening. The picture-book perfect beach stretched out in a crescent in front of the palm trees, but there was something odd about it. In the middle of it stood a huge, canopied stage, a massive PA system and a gigantic lighting rig. It was like a minute Glastonbury Festival, with the subtle difference that there was no one there, apart from the odd technician pottering about checking things. Yet the First Ever BVI Music Festival was due to start at any moment, so we set up camp on the beach and then ambled among the stalls, which were already up and running, selling rum punch, commemorative T-shirts and goat soup.

What followed was, for us, the nearest to paradise it would have been possible to get. All afternoon, a succession of acts from Tortola and the neighbouring islands took the opportunity to show what they could do on a big stage, as the audience gradually began to swell. Yet there were two big differences between this and any other festival. Firstly, in contrast to the UK, where you'd normally run a mile to avoid a succession of amateur local bands, the music (soul, gospel but predominantly reggae) was absolutely brilliant, this being a part of the world where music is taken seriously and musicians perform with genuine rhythm and feeling. And secondly, far from sitting in a sea of mud and litter, we were simply actually sitting in the sea, full stop. Bobbing about in the warm water and sipping Painkillers, in fact. *Mon Dieu!*

By the time Maxi Priest arrived, there had been a daringly risqué fashion show and a very long build-up hosted by a compère whose mastery of the single *entendre* would certainly have had Dave the taxi driver on his knees begging for his soul. It was pitch dark, the patch of beach in front of the stage was now full and we stood out a mile as virtually the only tourists. Whoopie! And Maxi, dressed from head to foot in Persil White, put on the sort of brutal reggae attack that his bland chart singles would never have led you to expect. The bass tones carried for miles and the light show was like the Aurora Borealis, while Maxi's diminutive rapper could probably have been heard back at home in Brixton, England, from where, mind-bogglingly, the band had travelled for the show. Well, to the good folk of Tortola, London is an exotic location, and they demonstrated their appreciation appropriately.

For the final encore, Maxi Priest invited a few selected members of the audience up onto the stage. Strangely, these audience members were all extremely beautiful women, and out of this grew, over the next couple of days, an island rumour which may or may not have been true, but I hope it was, because it's nice to fantasise about. Allegedly, according to the lady who ran the food stall on the beach at Jost Van Dyck, the island which we visited the next day, her sister, who was one of the stage invitees, was ushered into the wings by Maxi Priest's wife.

"Good evening," said Mrs Maxi, "Maxi and I have been observing you from the stage and we wondered whether you would like to sleep with us tonight?"

"Oh, yes, yes," I gagged, "and did she?"

"Ah, that would be telling," came the reply, complete with inscrutible wink.

By the following evening, there was no sign that the First Ever BVI Music Festival had ever taken place and it might have been tempting to view it as a dream, except that I have the T-shirt to prove that it wasn't. Occasionally, I wear it out in the middle of the UK winter in the hope that someone will say, "Blimey, you went to the First Ever BVI Music Festival, aren't you lucky?" but so far nobody has.

Depressingly, we made the mistake, the next evening, of entering an establishment which was an American-run hotel /restaurant complete with, naturally, its own generator, toadyish staff and ridiculous prices. Each beer cost five dollars, the same as a Shell Museum breakfast, so I didn't get drunk enough to do what I really should have done, which was to stand on a table and shout, "You bastards, you're killing Egberth." Instead, we listened in dumbfounded horror to two "beauty consultants" from Essex called Sharon and Tracy being clumsily chatted up by some middle-aged smoothie New Zealanders who claimed to be pilots. Sharon and Tracy said that Tortola was all right but that they'd rather be in Ibiza. Then they all went off together.

At the harbour on Jost van Dyck was a bar called Foxy's which is definitely the place to be on New Year's Eve. According to Foxy (who composed an instant calypso in our honour, making lots of false assumptions based on the fact that we said we came from England), on December 31st, his bar is the place to find Ron and Keith from the Rolling Stones, as well as Richard Branson. We reached Jost van Dyck by means of a ferry on which we were the only passengers, there and back. When we asked how it could be that, wherever we went, we were the sole tourists, the response made complete sense: Next week is the first week of the Hurricane Season. Fine.

Now then, Smuggler's Cove. Come off it. Anywhere called Smuggler's Cove is bound to be a vile theme park. I was almost tempted not to go there at all, so unpromising was the name. Whatever else it was, it couldn't be a real Smuggler's Cove, could it? And the journey there began unpromisingly, taking us right through the middle of the very "resort" which was ruining the livelihood of Egberth and the rest.

Before long, however, the hire jeep (a left-hand-drive model, driven on the left hand side of the road, a peculiar sensation, to say the least) was bumping its way down an almost invisible rocky road through sub-tropical rain forest. When we emerged onto the beach of Smugglers Cove, we realised that we truly had found paradise. Blah blah blah, deserted golden sands, palm trees, azure sea, coral reefs, well, there we were, that's what it was.

Of all things you wouldn't have expected to find at Smuggler's Cove, a beach bar would have been Number One, but there was one. Clearly ravaged by years of hurricanes, it looked vaguely Cuban, and there was a reason for that. Bob Denniston, the 82-year old proprietor, invited us to tap what appeared to be the solid stone structure and we realised that it was made of plywood, constructed, as Bob explained, specially for the filming of the 1989 version of Hemingway's "Old Man And The Sea", starring Anthony Quinn. But what on earth was that inside it? It was a white 1966 Lincoln Continental, the very one that was used to transport the Queen round Roadtown, the island's capital, when she visited on the occasion of her Silver Jubilee in 1977 and Bob volunteered to be the chauffeur. How it was actually driven to Smuggler's Cove remains a mystery, but it's there.

Bob, who was one of the island's earliest radio hams and used to warn of hurricanes in the days before satellites, operated a little Honesty Bar because, he said, he wasn't there that often and even when he was, he preferred to sit and shoot the breeze with anyone around, rather than act as barman.

But how did we get a beer? Simple. We had to delve into a cobwebby back room, past a rubber shark dangling on a string, and help ourselves to a bottle of Carib from the fridge, placing our dollar bills onto a plate on the bar. Then we could go and drink it in the sea. Funnily enough, said Bob, the people most likely to skip off without paying were those (by definition rich tourists) staying in the resorts. Well, *quelle surprise.*

The Old Man and the Sea, plus Lincoln Continental

The thing about Tortola was that hardly a minute passed without an adventure of some sort or other. For example, when we visited the "Baths" (a series of difficult-to-negotiate boulders and rock pools on Virgin Gorda), we stumbled into a photo shoot for an Italian calendar featuring a staggeringly beautiful girl (well, she made me stagger) modelling a bikini made of spirals of wire. It would have been rude not to stop and stare for a while, so fascinating were her nipples. I have a photo of this, and you haven't. Nonetheless, I'm going to be keeping a closer-than-usual eye on the market stalls this Autumn.

Almost within view of our cottage lay a venue, the like of which I sincerely believe exists nowhere else in the world. Please bear with me while I attempt to describe Bomba's Shack.

At first sight, you could be forgiven for thinking it was an unlit bonfire. Constructed entirely of driftwood, it looked so unlike an actual building that we passed it several times before realising that it was a bar. Completely open to the elements, standing forlornly on the beach, it looked as if it had long since been abandoned, rather like a shipwreck. Only, as we discovered, it wasn't only ships that got wrecked at Bomba's Shack.

Luckily, we had been warned. The various accounts left behind in the diary by previous holidaymakers were quite explicit: Try Bomba's punch, yes, but take it steady. One gentlemen had plainly had his vacation ruined and had spent at least three days of it in bed, recovering from a Bomba's Full Moon Party.

As we were there at the tail end of the season, Bomba's appeared disappointingly quiet. There were no special parties and most nights it seemed to be closed, until, during the last day, I noticed a poster advertising a barbecue for that evening. The perfect opportunity to savour Bomba's delights!

Up at Turtle Dove, something unexpected had happened. We suddenly found we had neighbours, up the hill in the next cottage, a young American couple called Stan and Kelly. We decided to ask them if they'd like to accompany us to Bomba's and they seemed keen. You do realise the importance of restraint, we asked? Yes, of course.

In Bomba's, there was a not very good DJ limbering up and one or two American couples who had walked up from the "resort" at Long Bay, looking for some action. Things were quiet, so there was time to have a good look round. The décor consisted of hundreds and hundreds of tatty discarded bras and knickers, dangling on nails from the low rafters. There was no way of avoiding brushing them with your head as you walked around on the sand floor. It didn't really bear thinking about, but after even the very first Bomba's punch, you pretty well didn't care about anything very much.

All over the outside and the inside of the construction, there were slogans painted, similar in appearance to those at the nearby Shell Museum, but rather different in tone:

"Visitor come to Full Moon Party to fight will be departed or throne in jale. Absolutly no fighting."

It wasn't until later that I began to understand why people might want to fight. A few minutes spent observing the bar began to explain Bomba's Shack's reputation for outrageous behaviour. Every time anyone ordered a punch, the large beaker would be filled up almost to the brim from a jug containing neat rum laced with Bomba's renowned "secret ingredients". The secret of these ingredients could well be deduced from one of the other prominent items on the menu: Mushroom tea.

Bomba's Shack. No naked flame, please.

On the wall by the bar was a poster offering a free T-shirt to any laydeez willing to take off their tops and bras. You might think that not many people would take up this offer, but that would reckon without the power of Bomba's punch. Just adjacent to the poster was Bomba's Polaroid collection, which demonstrated rather unappetisingly that the number of T-shirt winners was not inconsiderable.

Before setting out, Birgit and I had actually had a conversation in which we agreed to follow the advice of previous sufferers and go easy on the punch. Unfortunately, we hadn't conveyed that message to Stan with sufficient urgency. He ordered a round, and then another, and then another. Three Bomba's specials were enough to make me exceedingly mellow and almost, but not quite, willing to throw caution to the winds. I realised I had to keep my wits about me, because Birgit was becoming the centre of attention for several of the very good-looking, dreadlocked locals who liked to teach the tourists how to dance. I restricted myself to standing on the edge of the dance floor, pretending to be an interested and un-jealous observer (I was seething).

Stan, however, had passed the Bomba point of no return. Downing mug after mug of deadly punch, he began to dance suggestively with a succession of women of various shapes, sizes and ages, allowing his hands to wander into places not normally explored in public. This eventually became too much for his ignored wife Kelly, who had already told me that this was their second attempt at a honeymoon, the first one having been abandoned on account of Stan's appalling behaviour. She strode onto the dance floor, inflicted Stan with a well-aimed knee in the groin and stormed out into the night. It was spectacular.

Have you noticed how many people I've carried home in this book? Well, here we went again. It was an hour before Birgit had escaped the attentions of her band of admirers, most of whom had plenty of creative reasons for trying to persuade her that I was a pretty feeble husband and that she really ought to go home with them. Then there was the little matter of removing Stan's hands from inside various foreign bras and lugging him back up the precipice to where the reception that awaited him was unlikely to have much to do with Turtle Doves.

His legs weren't functioning, so we literally had to pull him along

the road, supporting him under his armpits. As we went, he dribbled essence of Bomba down his shirt and onto the track. And
all the time he gibbered abjectly:

"Oh fuck, what have I done? I was dancin' kinda sexual with
those women and now Kelly will never forgive me. How come
you guys have been married for twenty years and I can't even
manage two?"

We left Stan on his porch and allowed him to add his retching
sounds to the nocturnal chorus of frogs croaking and crickets
chirupping. The owners later Emailed us to say that he hadn't
been seen for the next three days and that Bomba had, true to
form, destroyed Stan's honeymoon and probably his marriage
as well.

We had to go home. Seeing the airport in daylight, we realised
that it was being modernised and extended in order to
accommodate big airliners which will be able to fly there direct
from Europe and the USA. This will mean that more and more
"resorts" will be built and that the genuine character of the island
will dwindle in the face of mass tourism. It is tempting to think
of going back, but I just couldn't bear to find Egberth's restaurant
and museum closed down, Bomba's collapsed into the sea and a
metalled road leading to Smuggler's Cove.

So I'll just live with my memories, thank you very much.

Aaaah.

Epilogue:

Echo Beach

It may be hard to believe, but I have, in fact, had plenty of uneventful, uniformly pleasurable holidays. Still, when pushed, everyone has just one favourite place in the whole wide world (or as much of the whole wide world as they have experienced). So now I'm going to tell you mine. Is it San Francisco? Venice? New York, maybe?

No, it's a tiny and almost unknown corner of Dorset, England.

The record producer Brendan Lynch likes the sound of the Rainstick. Primal Scream's "Vanishing Point" is liberally spattered with this strangely mournful swishing sound, whilst a particularly expansive example is to be found on "Friday Street" on Paul Weller's "Heavy Soul" album.

The sound of the Rainstick is a melancholy one. It's a noise which attracts a bizarre collection of addicts to the beach at Eype, just outside Bridport. In the case of the Rainstick, the sound is created by little stones tumbling through a network of twigs. At Eype, it's the waves breaking with metronomic regularity onto the steep bank of pebbles which form the shoreline.

So timeless and reliable is this sound that it tends to induce laughably frightening thoughts such as "How many pebbles are there on the beach?", progressing to "How many pebbles are there in the world?", "How many waves have washed up here?" and "Will there ever come a day when no waves will wash up here?" All thoughts which may or may not cross the minds of the small but dedicated number of people who, rain or shine, winter or summer, day or night, can be found sitting on the pebble bank, staring out to sea for hours on end.

What it is about certain places which gives them the power to mesmerise in this way? In the week I spent at Eype, rain fell ceaselessly for 72 hours and it was shrouded in fog for the rest of the time. Yet the (well-hidden) caravan park was full, the campsite was full, the B & Bs were full and no one showed any discontent or desire to leave. They must have been regulars, since it takes a real effort to get there. The lane is so winding and narrow that some people assume they're on the wrong road and turn back; anyone attempting to approach on foot has to negotiate steep, tortuous cliff paths.

One afternoon, I was stopped by a middle-aged gentleman who pretended he wanted to ask the way. It turned out that he knew exactly where he was. He introduced himself as being a Russian poet from Leningrad and, within moments, had produced from his rucksack a slim hardback book containing his own poems, all dedicated specifically to this small stretch of Dorset coastline.

Under other circumstances, the sentimental pidgin English would have been hilarious; as it was, the almost spiritual sincerity shone through so brightly that I read them avidly, pretending to know something about literature as I poured praise on them. Each poem had also been painstakingly translated into Russian. When I asked Leonid whether the book was on sale in Russia, he was amazed. "No, no, it has costed me much money." He hailed a passing walker to take a picture of me studying his literary work.

Leonid is by no means the only one to find Eype beach artistically inspirational. The African master drummer Noah Messomo holds highly atmospheric drum workshops here ("turn right", say the directions) and the artist John Skinner leads beach sculpture sessions. The singer and songwriter Polly Harvey is specifically inspired by these very waves and pebbles. Look how many of her songs reflect the power of water.

One night, at 1 a.m., we met in the lane a woman called Fiona and her young daughter, who had driven that day all the way from Rotherham. Their husband and father had deserted them ten days earlier and they'd chosen Eype beach as the place to "find themselves". Overcome with emotion as they told their story, they nonetheless were obviously gaining in strength and determination from their pilgrimage. They had two Rotweilers. "Don't trust them," said Fiona. "They don't like men."

The next night, I came over all sentimental myself. I had stumbled in the dark along the cliffs to the Anchor Inn at Seatown (just keep the Rainstick noises to your left, you can't go wrong), attracted by some musical tones. It turned out to be a friendly folk singer called Ken Watkins. Fed up with playing the acoustic standards requested by the crowd, he suddenly stopped.

"Jesus, I love this place," he cried, and launched himself into a perfect version of Richard Thompson's hardly-possible-to-play "Beeswing". The lump in my throat was almost unbearable.

Even in the middle of the night, there are figures hunched up on the top of the pebble bank. With their Hurricane lamps and their Thermoses, the dedicated shore fishermen of Eype spend most of their lives there. They never seem to catch anything, so what are they doing? It's obvious: They are composing songs, writing poems and discovering the true meaning of life.

The Rolling Stones, live at Eype.

Glossary

A guide to the exciting places mentioned in this book.

Abergavenny
An ideal place to play Twenty Questions.

Aldershot
Shot - that's appropriate, because the place is full of squaddies.

Amsterdam
*Visit Amsterdam for its canals, museums and tulips, **not** its Coffee Shops and red light area.*

Austin
Not only a make of car, but also the Live Music Capital Of The World.

Avignon
*It has a **pont**, upon which you can dance.*

Barcelona
Gothic, but forever besmirched by a horrible song by Freddy Mercury.

Basingstoke
From a distance, it looks like Frankfurt. Best viewed from a distance.

Bayonne
In my old French text book, there was a really exciting story about smugglers in Bayonne.

Beccles
Has a very good branch of Somerfields.

Berlin
Famous for its doughnut industry.

Bernkastel
Contrary to myth, it does not have 23 Town Halls.

Bilbao
You can sail there from Portsmouth, if you have a lot of time to spare.

Bognor
Nothing wrong with Bognor. The mini-golf is great.

Bolzano
Inspiration to anguished poets.

Bordeaux
The wine is probably really good, if you understand wine.

Brecon
Or "Brec", as we, its friends, call it.

Bridport
Hang around long enough and you'll eventually experience a PJ Harvey warm-up show.

Bremen
Home of some animals who pretend to be musicians. Makes a change from musicians pretending to be animals.

Brighouse
The place to get brassed off.

Brussels
There's a horrible little pissing bloke.

Calais
Shit - this must mean we're nearly home.

Cardiff
I once saw 10cc and Thin Lizzy live at Cardiff Castle.

Châteleaudren
Do not on any account ever go there.

Chelmsford
Has a hidden delight.

Cherbourg
Shit - this must mean we're nearly home.

Clacton
Fantastic in the middle of Winter when there's no one there.

Clapham
The urine puddle capital of the world.

Clun
Don't be disgusting.

Coburg
Just one letter away from an actor in the Magnificent Seven.

Copenhagen
Very important warning: If you ask for a hot dog with no mustard, they'll give you double mustard.

Crickhowell
Surrounded by sheep and SAS officers.

Dax
Just one letter away from a brand of washing powder.

Dijon
Where they make that stuff that they use so much of in Copenhagen.

Dorchester
Thomas Hardy called it Casterbridge. Was he dyslexic?

East Kilbride
The end of the world.

Echternach
Yes, but can you pronounce it?

Eckernförde
Yes, but can you pronounce it?

Elmshorn
How can an elm have a horn?

Engelberg
Angel mountain. Aaaaaah!

Eype
Ev'rybody must get stoned.

Farnborough
Spookily, just next to Fleet, not only alphabetically but also geographically.

Fleet
Spookily, just next to Farnborough, not only alphabetically but also geographically.

Frankfurt
From a distance, it looks just like Basingstoke.

Fredericksburg
It's not in Germany, it's in Texas Hill Country.

Frocester
Home to millions of Roman coins.

Fulda
Fairy-tale German town No.1.

Galway
My children once made £8.55 by standing on a street corner in Galway and singing excerpts from the Lion King.

Garmisch-Partenkirchen
David Vine can't pronounce it.

Gatwick
Dementia.

Geneva
I know my opinion of Geneva shouldn't be coloured by the fact that I trod in some dog shit. But it is.

Granada
"After a day in Granada, you will have to stay for several more because the queue for the Alhambra is so bloody long."

Great Yarmouth
Home of the Hullabaloos.

Grindelwald
David Vine can't pronounce it.

Hebden Bridge
You stand out if you aren't altenative.

Honfleur
The thinking person's Le Havre.

Horning
Sounds rude, doesn't it?

Hungerford
I've done things in Hungerford that are best forgotten.

Innsbruck
No doubt it's beautiful, but I associate it with snoring, farting and cheesy feet.

Interlaken
David Vine can't pronounce it.

Jost van Dyck
Certainly an oil painting.

Kiel
It has a university, just like Keele.

Kirkwall
To visit it, you have to cross the Pentland Firth. So don't visit it.

Krakow
If you meet that toilet attendant, tell her to piss off.

Le Havre
Shit - this must mean we're nearly home.

Lerwick
The Big City.

Lucerne
How can this possibly be a type of grain?

Lugo
Only one letter away from a board game.

Luxembourg
"The Station Of The Stars". Ah, happy days.

Magaluf
You lookin' at me?

Majorca
Let's get this straight: People go here voluntarily?

Mantes-La-Jolie
Jolie it isn't.

Madrid
Not a good place to be when it's hot. And that's always.

Mirandela
I daren't go back because it might turn out to be horrible.

Monmouth
Or "Mon", as we, its friends, call it.

Mont de Marsan
The Clash, The Damned and The Jam. Honest!

Montpellier
The swishest trams in Europe, populated exclusively by crusties.

Munich
Anywhere with this amount of beer is okay by me.

Münster
Probably quite nice but all it brings to mind is naked people in saunas.

Newbury
Pass.

Newtown
No, the Welsh one.

New Orleans
Get your mojo working on those 'gators.

Nürnberg
Their sausages are quite a trial.

Odiham
I once applied for a job here. I wonder how different life would have turned out if ... (etc., etc,)

Orkney
The Dallas of the North.

Palma
Only one letter away from a type of ham.

Paris
The German word for a condom is a Pariser. That's interesting, isn't it?

Porthcawl
Tiger Woods would like it.

Porto
I was going to write a chapter about Portuguese drivers but never got round to it.

Potter Heigham
Mind your head on that bridge.

Puttgarten
"Now you walk with your feets."

Ramsau
Piss off!

Reedham
Norfolk and good.

Rochdale
Famous for ... Cyril Smith? Lisa Stansfield?

Rothenburg ob der Tauber
Fairy-tale German town No. 2.

Ronda
Fairy-tale Spanish town No.1. (Sorry, there isn't a No. 2).

Santa Ponsa
Don't go there. Ever.

San Antonio
King of the Wild Frontier.

Santiago de Compostela
Allegedly very beautiful, if you're sober.

Saunton
If only it hadn't been for that horrible vicar.

Schladming
It's a railway junction.

Schöningen
This used to be an interesting place in the East-West German border. Now there is no East-West German border, it isn't interesting any more.

Seville
If only you could get there, the oranges would probably be quite nice.

Shawford
Victor Meldrew died here. Really.

Shetland
My Little Pony.

Solihull
Populated only by pensioners.

Sowerby Bridge
Bleak, industrial.

Stalham
Scampi and Slipknot.

St Jean de Luz
Remember that French smuggling story? Well, this town featured in it as well.

Stonewall
Luscious Jackson.

Todmorden
Shudder!

Tortola
Only two letters away from a Mexican snack.

Tours
As long as they aren't Guided ones.

Tralee
Roses are red.

Trier
That's Tree-ur.

Troyes
That's as in un, deux, ..., not Helen of ...

Ulm
Round and round the garden.

Uzès
Useless, more like.

Valenciennes
A horrible place which shares a first syllable with Valladolid.

Valladolid
A horrible place which shares a first syllable with Valenciennes.

Viana do Castelo
Do you know the parrot joke?

Vias
Home of Gratuitous Balloon Offering.

Virgin Gorda
Nothing to do with Dutch cheese, despite being only two letters away.

Wangerooge
Watch how you pronounce it.

Waterville
Not Waterford, okay?

Winchester
If you mention that you come from Winchester, any foreign person will immediately say, "Ah! Where the guns come from." But any British person will immediately burst into song: "Winchester Cathdral, la la la la la". None of them have any idea about Winchester.

Wroxham
Where you can get your Wrox off.

Würzburg
Fairy-tale German town No. 3.

Zacopane
You can toboggan down the mountain, even in summer.

Also by Oliver Gray:

VOLUME

A Cautionary Tale of Rock and Roll Obsession

Here's what the critics had to say about **VOLUME**:

"It's honest and very, very funny. You'll love it."
- The News, Portsmouth, UK.

"I've never read a book like it. It's really, really enjoyable.
You just can't put it down."
-Richard Cartridge, BBC Radio, UK.

"The anecdotes make better reading than a holiday novel."
- Good Times magazine, Germany.

"Sadly humorous and ceaselessly interesting."
- Amplifier magazine, USA.

Available from all good bookshops.

Sarsen Press

ISBN: 1-897609-81-7